STICKY

MARKETING

STICKY

MARKETING

Why everything in
marketing has changed
and what to do about it

Grant Leboff

KoganPage

LONDON PHILADELPHIA NEW DELHI

Sticky Marketing is a trade mark of Grant Leboff
Problem Map and Problem Maps are registered trade marks of Grant Leboff

First published in Great Britain and the United States in 2011 by Kogan Page Limited

120 Pentonville Road
London N1 9JN
United Kingdom
www.koganpage.com

1518 Walnut Street, Suite 1100
Philadelphia PA 19102
USA

4737/23 Ansari Road
Daryaganj
New Delhi 110002
India

© Grant Leboff, 2011

The right of Grant Leboff to be identified as the author of this work has been asserted by him in accordance with the Copyright, Designs and Patents Act 1988.

ISBN   978 0 7494 6050 1
E-ISBN   978 0 7494 6051 8

British Library Cataloguing-in-Publication Data

A CIP record for this book is available from the British Library.

Library of Congress Cataloging-in-Publication Data

Leboff, Grant.
   Sticky marketing : why everything in marketing has changed and what to do about it / Grant Leboff.
        p. cm.
   Includes index.
   ISBN 978-0-7494-6050-1 – ISBN 978-0-7494-6051-8   1. Marketing. 2. Internet marketing. 3. Information technology–Social aspects. I. Title.
   HF5415.L362 2010
   658.8–dc22
                                                        2010031893

Typeset by Saxon Graphics Ltd, Derby
Printed in the UK by CPI Antony Rowe

BRIEF CONTENTS

CONTENTS

LIST OF FIGURES AND TABLES

API	Application Programming Interfaces
CEO	Chief executive officer
CEP	Customer engagement points
CMR	Customer managed relationships
CRM	Customer relationship management
FD	Financial director
GPS	Global positioning system
MD	Managing director
ROE	Return on engagement
ROI	Return on investment
RSS	Really Simple Syndication
SEO	Search engine optimization
UGC	User-generated content
USP	Unique selling point or unique selling proposition

"Grant Leboff has carefully considered the current approach of most organizations to marketing their products and suggests that companies must no longer 'shout at' or mass market their products to a wide range of potential customers, but use word of mouth and social media to gain an outstanding reputation.

Grant has shown his clients that this approach even enables the producers of 'boring' products to boost their reputation and sales by using new forms of communication with their potential customers, such as YouTube. If you follow Grant's advice I am sure that you should see an improvement in your company's reputation and sales.

I recommend that you take a look at Grant's new book..." **Nigel Adams, Programme Director BSc Business Enterprise, University of Buckingham Business School**

"*Sticky Marketing* is one of those books that captures perfectly how effective marketing has changed. If you want a no-nonsense insight on how to engage effectively with your customers and would be customers this should be on your reading list." **Duncan Cheatle, Founder, The Supper Club, www.thesupperclub.net, The UK's foremost club for high growth, innovative entrepreneurs**

"I first heard Grant speak at a networking event and was struck by the eminent common sense of what he had to say. In this book Grant has given us a view of how the world is changing and written a very simple, clear and practical guide as to how marketing strategy has to adapt in order to respond to the new empowered consumer. Whether your business is – global or local – *Sticky Marketing* is relevant. **Walter Zanre, Managing Director, Filippo Berio UK Ltd**

"There is a gap between the latest marketing philosophies (eg behaviour economics) and what marketers do every day. In *Sticky Marketing*, Leboff makes sense of cutting edge marketing thought as well as the latest technological innovations in marketing in that plain talking, anecdote rich way that we've enjoyed in his public speaking appearances for years." **Steve Barton, Global Brand Partner at OgilvyOne Worldwide and inaugural President of WOMMA UK (the word of mouth marketing association in the UK)**

"Marketing has changed in very complex ways. Grant explains the changes in ways that are easy to comprehend. He also shares what you need to do to succeed in this new world, and communicates this in a powerful, entertaining, and motivational way. Step one is reading this book!" **Dave Clarke, CEO, NRG-networks.com**

"Finally, a book that brings marketing into the new world. *Sticky Marketing* is a must for all marketers and business owners. Grant lays out in a very sensible and practical way what marketing in the new economy should be about, and gives some very clear examples to illustrate his points. Whatever your industry, whatever size your business is, if you want to succeed where others are failing, then read this book." **Steve Gilroy, CEO, Vistage International (UK) Ltd**

"In an era of information overload, engaging with customers becomes critical. Grant Leboff's book provides a critical perspective on marketing and addresses topical subjects such as social media and behavioural targeting. An excellent read for marketing practitioners as well as scholars." **Dr Dan Alex Petrovici, Lecturer in Marketing, Kent Business School**

"In the Digital Age many have still to cotton on to the fact that it is not about technology, it is about a shift in culture and a shift in the way transactions are achieved. The role of business leaders has changed. Transactional leaders are being left behind, while leaders who focus on the customer's lives, challenges and needs are building 'followers'. Grant has an incredible sales and marketing brain. In the book he shares practical tips and skills that will help business leaders to shift their thinking and build communication strategies that are right for now." **Penny Power, Founder, ecademy.com**

"Grant Leboff's new book comes at an important time when marketers have the once-in-a-lifetime opportunity to reclaim the boardroom and put the customer at the very top of the business agenda. As such *Sticky Marketing* makes the compelling case for creating lasting value in the eyes of 'more demanding' customers who live in the 'more demanding' world." **Darrell Kofkin, Chief Executive, Global Marketing Network**

PART 01

PROLOGUE

What the Sex Pistols taught me about marketing

It was a mild autumn day in 1999. I was in the UK, in Brighton, at a recording studio belonging to a friend of mine, Paul Mex.[1] We were having a chat about the state of the music industry, because in the summer of that year Shawn Fanning had started Napster, a music file-sharing site, giving people the ability to share music with each other all around the world.

The music industry later had Napster closed down. At the time, however, there were many people who were infuriated that consumers were now sharing music across the internet, for free. The music industry's business model was based on the fact that they controlled the distribution of music and charged the public to access it. In 1999, this was mainly by way of CDs.

We were having a discussion about the future of the music industry, and how they were going to approach this new development. While we were having this debate, Paul suddenly stopped the conversation and told me he wanted me to listen to a recording he had. At the back of the studio was a cupboard full of tapes, records, cables etc, and Paul rummaged in there for what seemed like an age. He eventually returned waving a cassette. He sat me down and told me to have a listen.

He explained that it was a tape of a live phone-in with Paul Cook and Steve Jones from the Sex Pistols, Paul's favourite band, which took place in the summer of 1978 on KSJO Radio in the United States. He pressed play on the tape recorder and we sat back and started to listen. About two minutes into the recording, Paul indicated that the section he wanted me to hear was coming up.

At that moment, a woman listener came on the air. She was decidedly unimpressed with the Sex Pistols and had phoned in to tell them so. She was given her opportunity to speak and started, 'I just wanted to say that I don't think the Sex Pistols have any right to cut down the Queen until they learn how to be musicians first.' At that point Steve Jones interrupted, replying: 'It's got nothing to do with music, you silly cow!' Paul then stopped the cassette player.

I looked at him, puzzled. 'Did you get it?', Paul asked.

'I think so', I replied, decidedly unsure.

Paul made an MP3 file of the interview. I saved it to my desktop and every so often I would have a listen. As broadband became ubiquitous, and the internet was having a greater influence on our lives, Steve Jones's comment back in 1978 seemed to resonate with me more and more. Eventually, I could not get it out of my mind. I soon realized that this one comment seemed to summarize much of what I was trying to say in the speeches I was presenting, and in the work I was undertaking with clients.

It may have been a flippant comment made 12 years before the invention of the internet, but Steve Jones had opened my eyes to what I observed was happening at the dawn of the 21st century and he was right... 'It's got nothing to do with music, you silly cow!'

Sticky marketing is not about how to conduct an e-mail marketing campaign or the intricacies of search engine optimization (SEO). Rather, it is a new way of thinking. This book will present a narrative as to how and why the old rules of marketing are no longer relevant. It will uncover the 'new rules' by which companies must now operate in order to be successful.

By changing their mindset and adopting these new principles, businesses will be able to adapt their marketing in order to be effective in this web-enabled technological age. *Sticky Marketing* will explain how companies can become attractive, which in turn will lead prospects to their door. It will detail how to create competitive advantage in a world where customers seemingly have a plethora of choices, and where standing out appears to be increasingly difficult. Ultimately, *Sticky Marketing* will explain the principles, and the steps that need to be taken, in order to become 'sticky'. In so doing, a business will emerge with which prospects and customers alike will want to engage. The result is that a company will acquire one of the most precious resources available, and the one that all companies require in order to be successful. That is: customer attention.

PART 02

SETTING

THE SCENE

Printing press to internet

> When I became President in 1993, there were only fifty sites on the worldwide web – unbelievable – fifty. When I left office, the number was three hundred and fifty million and rising. (President Bill Clinton, 2001[1])

As alluded to by President Clinton, it is the pace at which change has taken place since the invention of the internet that has made understanding its effects so difficult. Many established companies failed to grasp quickly enough how the landscape was altering. Consequently, they have been left behind by new companies that have filled the void.

For example, Yellow Pages was a concept and brand known throughout the world for over 100 years.[2] In whichever country you lived, it was often your first point of reference when looking for a product, service or supplier. Quite simply, Yellow Pages dominated search. Surely, therefore, any of the major companies that owned Yellow Pages were in the best position to establish themselves as the major search tool on the internet. In the UK, Yellow Pages was owned by British Telecom,[3] a huge company with vast resources. Yet, it was Google that became the major search brand online: a company with no history, launched in 1998 from a garage in California by two computer graduates.[4]

Similarly, *Loot* (Magazine), first published in the UK in 1985,[5] was a market leader if you had unwanted items that you wished to sell. Therefore, one could argue, certainly in the UK, that it was in the best position to establish this market online. However, it was eBay, founded

10 years later in 1995,[6] that established itself as the major provider of this service.

Whether it is Amazon, usurping all major book retailers, or the failure of any large telecom provider to be the first to develop a service like SKYPE, now the biggest carrier of international calls in the world,[7] there is a litany of examples of established companies failing to grasp the opportunities, or seeing the risks to their business, that the revolution in technology and communication has brought.

It is the old analogy of the frog in water that is put on to boil. As the water heats up, it cannot ascertain the subtle changes in its surroundings. By the time it realizes the water is boiling, it is too late. Similarly, many companies have failed to grasp the changes that are taking place around them. They have tried to bolt the internet onto their existing business model, failing to realize that the internet is not merely a new communications vehicle, but rather represents a fundamental change in the rules of engagement.

Sticky Marketing explains how the rules have changed, and the new principles that companies need to embrace in order to thrive in the current business environment.

The development of communication

It is unbelievable to think that when Bill Clinton was being inaugurated as the 42nd President of the United States, there were only 50 sites on the internet. In fact, it was only in December 1990[8] that the first web client–server communication took place over the internet. Yet, despite its relatively short existence, Sir Tim Berners-Lee's creation is now proving itself to be the biggest revolution in communication since the invention of print.

Having invented the technique of printing in the 1450s,[9] it was Johann Gutenberg who published the first real book, a version of the Bible. Gutenberg introduced the world to the first one-to-many mass medium of communication. In other words, from the pen of one, the written word could be distributed to the many. This allowed for the wider dissemination of knowledge.

Printing enabled people to publish their ideas throughout the world. Once the power of this communication was unleashed, life was never the same again. The Protestant Reformation, the Renaissance and the Scientific Revolution are unlikely to have occurred without printing allowing ideas to spread. Thus, the revolution in communication, signified by Gutenberg's first printed book, helped to change the course of history.

Of course, there have been many other developments in the world of communication that have impacted on our lives. The 20th century saw dramatic changes in communication as new inventions started to affect the way we live. The influence of cinema, radio and television[10a, 10b, 10c] can in no way be underestimated. In its heyday, families would schedule their week around the popular TV programmes of the day. It was these shows that also set the tone for many of the conversations that took place around the coffee machine at work the following morning. Cinema, radio and television, however, still represented the transmission of ideas from one to many.

It was print that changed all the rules, by making mass communication possible. The other developments merely made the one-to-many medium more efficient. For example, television made it possible to communicate with a much larger audience, simultaneously. However, although cinema, radio and, in particular, television did change the game of communication, they did not change the rules by which the game was played.

In other words, print allowed for the mass marketing of products via advertising, mail order catalogues and direct mail pieces. Using television, the mass marketing model may have reached a bigger audience than traditional direct mail. This was because many of the big TV shows would have larger audiences than an average direct mail campaign. One could also argue that having sound and pictures delivered directly into people's homes gave those communications greater influence, although this is certainly debatable. However, the reality is that the principles were the same. The audience were still passive receivers of communication, with no right of reply. These broadcasts were generated by those who had the money to utilize the distribution channels available.

Let me explain, using a tennis analogy: the game of tennis changed when players migrated from the old wooden racquets to those made of graphite.[11] The new racquets gave players power with unprecedented accuracy. The game became faster and the serve became harder to return. These developments undoubtedly changed the game. They did not, however, change the rules by which tennis was played.

Similarly, print was the revolution in communication because it changed the rules. It made mass communication and the spreading of ideas possible. Meanwhile, cinema, radio and television, like our graphite racquet, merely changed the game by creating an increasing variety of potent channels through which to reach the audience. The game may have become faster and more furious, but nevertheless, the rules of mass communication remained the same.

The invention of print and the other forms of one-to-many communication both changed the world in which we live and influenced the way our society has developed. However, the limitations of these forms of communication have been as important to our development as the benefits.

The limitations of traditional communication channels

Because these vehicles of communication are one to many, they did not allow for mass discussions to take place. Authors, producers and programme makers could put their message across to millions, but the majority of their audience did not have the means with which to reply. Of course, people could discuss a particular message with friends. Certain individuals, such as journalists, could react when writing reviews. Books, television programmes and films could even inspire other authors and creators to write something new in reaction or reply to a piece of work. However, the number of people who were able to respond and be heard was severely limited. The one-to-many form of communication in itself is not capable of facilitating a discussion.

For example, when the Beach Boys released their groundbreaking album, 'Pet Sounds', in 1966, individual journalists could write reviews and reactions to the album. Paul McCartney himself acknowledges that 'Sgt. Pepper's Lonely Hearts Club Band' was, in part, the Beatles' reaction to the 'Pet Sounds' album.[12] Meanwhile, although millions of music fans may have had one-to-one conversations regarding the record, they were unable to be heard by a wider audience. This left the average fan a mere passive observer in the discussions taking place between the few voices with the means to grab their attention.

This highlights another limitation of the one-to-many platform, in that distribution was in the hands of relatively few. Anyone could write a book or record a song, but without access to a publisher or record company and its distribution network, it was unlikely that many others would know of its existence.

Whether it was newspapers, films or TV, it was media conglomerates that owned the distribution channels necessary to reach a wider audience. Therefore, few voices would be heard. Meanwhile, those who had control over the distribution of the information exerted enormous influence on our lives. Certainly in the arts it was the big film, record and publishing companies, and those they employed, that chose which acts were financed and which were never to see the light of day. Without being signed by one of these large companies it was unlikely that an artist, author or filmmaker would have any success at all.

We can acknowledge the existence of pirate radio stations, independent filmmakers and underground magazines that have been successful. However, these are exceptions rather than the rule. In the main, those with the means of distribution were heard, with everyone else unable to communicate their message beyond friends, colleagues and family.

In business, companies would gain access to distribution through money. For example, a company could produce television or radio advertising and buy airtime. Alternatively, it was possible to design messages for newspapers, billboards and magazines and purchase space. Companies could also go to the expense of designing, printing and posting their own direct mail. Whatever the vehicle, without money, it was impossible to obtain distribution and, therefore, to be heard. Generally, it was the larger companies that could afford to take advantage of these tools of communication. Smaller businesses would have less access to the media, owing to lower budgets.

Consequently, our lives were shaped by the big media magnates and companies that could control the means of distribution and the large companies that had the money to buy access to that distribution network. In the main, the individual was reduced to being a passive recipient. While one-to-many communications inspired billions of one-to-one discussions between friends, family and colleagues, most people had no means by which to be heard beyond their immediate circle.

The internet's impact on communication

The creation of the internet is now changing all the rules of communication. As with the invention of print, it has radically altered the way in which we react to, and disseminate, information. Just as print was the first one-to-many form of communication, the internet is the first many-to-many medium.

No longer do individuals need to own a large media network or have access to money to be heard. Using the internet, anyone can broadcast their message. This, in turn, means that individuals are no longer reduced to the role of passive recipient. Everyone is now able to react to others' messages in real time. As this process escalates, a conversation ensues between tens, hundreds or even thousands of people, as comments and reactions can be added to a discussion on an ongoing basis. Thus the internet is capable of facilitating a dialogue between potentially millions of people in a way that no previous media outlet could.

While it is possible to use the internet as a one-to-many communication tool, it is impossible to prevent your audience from having a right to reply. Therefore, although many companies have tried to use the internet to broadcast their one-to-many messages, these have often turned into many-to-many communications, as empowered individuals take it upon themselves to exercise their right to react. For example, even if a company broadcasts its message without allowing a direct reply on that page, anybody can post a comment in a relevant forum, chat room, blog or on a social network.

Before the invention of the internet, the majority of the public had very few vehicles with which to voice an opinion. For example, we could write a letter to a newspaper column, but few would ever be published. Also, the time lag between writing and posting a comment, and it subsequently being received and printed, meant that often it would lose some of its potency.

Compare that with today, when we can send a message from our mobile phones, reacting immediately to a story we have just seen. Moreover, many of us now have our own distribution networks. Whether these are our friends on Facebook, connections on LinkedIn, subscribers to our blog or newsletter or followers on Twitter, an increasing number of us have a ready-made audience to which we can impart our thoughts and feelings. Media such as YouTube, iTunes, Squidoo and Dailymotion offer anyone the chance to distribute their message to a mass audience. The proliferation of digital technology has meant that individuals can now make video and audio recordings with relative ease. In other words, people can now voice their opinions and broadcast a message in written, audio and visual formats and enjoy immediate distribution with virtually no cost at all. What we have witnessed is the empowerment of the individual and the democratization of information.

For example, we no longer solely rely on the established news networks to deliver us information about current events. During the hotel terrorist attacks in Mumbai (November 2008), we received more potent and current information from people posting messages on Twitter, from the hotels that were under attack, than any news network could deliver. Similarly, some of the most powerful and interesting videos from the post-election demonstrations in Iran (June 2009) were posted on YouTube by participants.

Forums and discussion groups that proliferate on the internet invite us to comment and be heard. For example, while watching the 2009 inauguration of President Obama, there was an average of 4,000[13] status updates every minute through the CNN.com live Facebook feed. These were people commenting and reacting to each other's observations, in real time, throughout the entire broadcast.

This ease of distribution also means that we no longer react to information in the same way. We are often willing and able to share with our friends messages that we find particularly interesting or funny. Before the creation of the internet we might have torn an article out of a newspaper or magazine and shown it to a few select people, or mentioned a particular programme to a few friends. Now we can share content with our entire address book, or social network, at the touch of a button.

It is not just the ease with which we can contribute and distribute ideas that has empowered us. It is also the access to information provided by the internet that has been liberating. Before the internet, finding information was often a time-consuming, laborious and difficult process. Now, we can go online and find the knowledge that we require, almost immediately. Whether it is news, reviews, products, facts, instructions, schedules or reports, there are very few situations where we are unable to find the information we require.

However one chooses to define marketing, at its core is the communication of ideas. The internet is the biggest revolution in communication since the invention of print. This being the case, if the rules of communication have changed, doesn't it make sense that the rules of marketing must also change?

The internet's influence on global change

The internet has also helped accelerate other game-changing factors. There is no doubt that even before the internet, the world was becoming a smaller place. Trade amongst many nations was becoming increasingly free; for example, the creation of the Common Market,[14] which subsequently became the European Union, brought the nations of Western Europe closer together both politically and economically. Meanwhile, the fall of the Berlin Wall[15] had opened up the world and the phenomenon of globalization was emerging.[16]

However, the internet has broken down borders even further. We can now read newspapers, listen to radio and watch news broadcasts and TV programmes from many different countries. We can have discussions with people throughout the world via blogs and forums or through communities and social networks with common interests. In this way, information and ideas can now be shared globally with ease. We can also source products and services internationally. The internet means that geography is no longer the boundary it once was.

In order to save costs, technology has also made possible the outsourcing of labour to other places in the world. For example, you can staff a call centre in India and be taking calls from customers in the United States or United Kingdom. The internet makes it easier for people in different countries to access the same piece of information. Culturally, the internet is also breaking down barriers, as we are increasingly engaging with people from all corners of the earth. This has resulted in people becoming more comfortable dealing with other countries than perhaps they once were.

Technology has also made it easier for people to work for themselves. The capital outlay that was once necessary to start a business is no longer required. Online access is all you need. The internet, together with e-mail, allows you to engage and communicate with prospects and customers relatively inexpensively.

This has led to a proliferation of small businesses, with an increasing number appearing all the time. Not everyone today is an entrepreneur, although there are many more than there once were. However, with capital outlay no longer a barrier, and in a knowledge economy, people no longer see the need to work for others. This is especially true as one of the major reasons for seeking employment was job security. In today's market, this is something that even the biggest corporations do not seem to be able to offer in the way they once did. Big businesses still exist, but the dynamics of the marketplace have changed. Whereas in the 1970s or 1980s you might not have considered buying from a one-person business working from home, you probably would now.

In short, we live in a world where people have been empowered. Anyone can produce content relatively cheaply and easily and have the means with which it can be distributed. Companies, however small, can communicate directly with their customers in a way not previously possible. Meanwhile, consumers can now give direct feedback to companies, and perhaps more importantly, can talk to each other, cutting the company out of the communication completely. These peer-to-peer conversations have given the general population a voice they never had before.

Sticky Marketing takes into account the changes that we are experiencing. It provides a new set of rules for effective communications in a world which has been impacted by advancements in technology and the internet.

Customers have changed.

Communication has changed.

Marketing must change.

Sticky Marketing provides you with a compelling response to the change.

KEY-POINT SUMMARY

- The internet is the biggest revolution in communication since the invention of print. It is not merely a new communication vehicle but represents a fundamental change in the rules of engagement.

- The internet is the first many-to-many medium. It is capable of facilitating a dialogue between potentially millions of people in a way no previous media outlet could.

- Using the internet, anyone can broadcast their message. Therefore, individuals are no longer reduced to the role of passive recipient.

- Today, many individuals have their own distribution networks, whether these are friends on Facebook, connections on LinkedIn, subscribers to a blog or newsletter or followers on Twitter.

- The access to information that the internet provides is liberating. Information and ideas can now be shared globally with ease. Geography is no longer the barrier it once was.

- The internet has resulted in the empowerment of the individual and the democratization of information.

CHAPTER 02

Scarcity to abundance

As technology and the internet play a greater part in our lives, we are seeing a shift in the dynamics of scarcity and abundance. Think back to 1990, the year the first-ever communication took place over the internet.[1] At the time, most people probably thought that they had a lot of choice and access to information. Yet, relative to where we are today, this was not the case. For example, here are some of the ways in which UK consumers were limited in choice at that time:

- Sky TV was less than one year old, having started on 5 February 1989.[2] It had only one million subscribers, leaving virtually the entire UK population with a choice of only four terrestrial television channels.

- The European air industry was going through deregulation, a process that did not finish until 1 January 1993.[3] EasyJet was not to launch until 1995[4] and although Ryanair flew its first low-budget flight in 1986,[5] the choices in low-cost air travel that we enjoy today were not available.

- There were only two landline telephone providers, BT and Mercury, with the latter enjoying only 3.5%[6] share of the residential phone market. Therefore, almost everybody's telephone was provided by British Telecom.

- The only gas supplier was British Gas.[7] Full competition in the gas supply market did not exist until 1998.

- Full competition in the electricity supply market did not exist until 1999.[7]

- The financial services market had only been deregulated in 1986;[8] therefore, the array of choices we have today were only just starting to emerge.

In 1990, we had relatively little access to information:

- Only 1.14 million[9] people owned a mobile phone, representing only 1.9% of the UK population.[10]
- There was no SMS text messaging. This wasn't introduced until December 1992.[11]
- There was no internet and so it was not easy to find potential suppliers of products and services. Most of us relied on the Yellow Pages or specialist and trade magazines.
- The adoption of e-mail in business, and later by consumers, did not take place until providers like Demon launched in the UK in 1992 and AOL started to connect their proprietary e-mail systems to the internet in 1993.[12a, 12b]

So in 1990, compared with today, there was a scarcity of both choice and access to information. However, it was relatively easy to grab our attention at that time, as there were only four terrestrial TV channels in the UK. On coming home from work, many people would be switching to one of the four channels on their TV sets. Since 1990, viewing figures for the top 10 TV programmes in the UK have been in steady decline, as they have in other countries where the media have fragmented, such as the United States.[13] This has led to many reports indicating that television advertising is becoming less potent as a medium for communication. For example, in the McKinsey report 'Profiting from proliferation' it was estimated that by 2010 television advertising 'could be only 35 per cent as effective as it was in 1990 [14]'.

In the UK, in 1990, of the four terrestrial television channels available, only two were commercial stations. Therefore, if a company wanted to relay a message to the wider public, paying for advertising on one of these two channels was deemed good value for money, as it would reach an extremely wide audience. Moreover, viewers did not have the array of distractions and variety of channels to which to flick during the commercial breaks. Whether it was advertising on television, direct mail through your door or individuals calling on a telephone, essentially, companies would pay to shout messages at us. This proved an effective form of communication.

In a world before the internet, consumers did not have easy access to information. Therefore, while companies would shout to enable them to sell their products and services, consumers were prepared to listen. Where did you go to find out about a better mortgage product, the latest technology or a new service that might be available locally? In this environment, when direct mail shots were posted through your door, the telephone rang from a sales call or the advertising came on television, then, assuming it was well written and well put together, we were willing to pay attention. Although consumers were well aware that companies were trying to sell to them, these messages were often a valuable source of information. It was in their interest to give time to these messages as much as it was in the company's interest to create them.

In a world scarce of both choice and information, the old marketing model worked on an unwritten contract between company and consumer. A business would pay money to interrupt what we were doing and shout their message at us, but if the messages were well presented and of good quality, consumers were prepared to watch, listen or read, as there was value in it for them. Now, if you look at where we are today, there is an absolute reversal.

The abundance of choice and information

In most facets of our lives, rather than a scarcity of choice, we are now presented with an absolute abundance in almost everything. Whether it be food, clothes, suppliers for our business requirements or ways to spend our leisure time, we are usually faced with a plethora of options. Obviously there are exceptions. For example, there has traditionally been a shortage of housing stock in the United Kingdom. We also have the challenge of the limitations of many natural resources.

I sometimes think that a contributory factor to our cynicism about politics is the fact that it is one of the few areas of our lives where we are limited in our choice. For example, both the United Kingdom and

United States operate what is essentially a two-party system, limiting our alternatives. However, our normal experience in our day-to-day lives is having a vast array of options.

Not only do we have more choices than ever before, but the web gives us the wherewithal to identify them both locally and globally. For example, think about buying a television. Before the internet, you would most likely visit a few local stores in order to make a purchase. If the model you required was unavailable, it would have to be ordered and another visit to the shop would have to be made, often weeks later. Moreover, the selection on offer was often limited by what we saw on the shelves in the few places that served our locality.

Today, via the web, we have easy access to almost all the choices available. We are no longer limited by the stock that our local provider carries. In fact, in many cases, we can research, choose and pay for items and have them delivered within 24 hours, without ever leaving the comfort of our homes or offices.

The access to information that the internet provides allows us to compare products and services from a larger array of providers than previously possible, thus enabling us to make a more informed choice. Rather than physically having to make contact with every provider, today most of the information we require is at our fingertips. The abundance of both information and choice means that in most areas of our lives we are now confident that we will not only be able to find what we want, but that we will also be able to make the purchase at our convenience.

However, the one resource that has always been scarce, and has become increasingly so, is our time. We have a finite number of hours in any given day and it is widely accepted that technology has made our lives busier than ever before. People now attend to e-mails on the train, text friends while queuing and make telephone calls from their cars. The natural downtime that existed in the normal ebb and flow of life has all but disappeared.

With time so scarce, our lives so busy and an increasing number of messages and amount of information making demands upon us, we are having to become more efficient at screening out unwanted and unnecessary communications. It is this reality that has meant that our unwritten contract with those companies that are shouting at us has been broken.

How many people:

- regularly read their direct mail?
- take cold calls and are pleased to receive them?
- frequently watch and remember TV commercials?
- don't flick to other channels when advertising messages appear?
- watch their programming on digital recorders or online, enabling them to bypass advertising?

Many companies still perceive that there is value in shouting at their potential customers as a way of encouraging them to buy their products or services. The problem for these companies is that there is little value in consumers receiving this information any more.

The 'shouting' lost its value

Although it is impossible to prove, I have substantial anecdotal evidence that years ago many of us would have a cupboard in the hallway, or a drawer in the kitchen, where we would store useful direct mail pieces and leaflets. With access to information so difficult, it seemed worth while keeping literature that might be useful at a later date. With the possible exception of takeaway menus, who keeps this material now? With all the knowledge that we require available to us at the stroke of a key, most direct mail finds its way straight into the bin.

As customers, we have all been empowered. We are now confident that when we require a product or service, we will be able to find it and make a purchase. Previously, we were prepared to put up with the shouting and unwanted messages because they often proved to be a useful source of information. Frequently we did receive value from these communications. When messages were not useful, we were fairly ambivalent about them. However, today this has changed. We have plenty of access to the information we require, which we can obtain at our convenience, rather than when it suits a company to shout at us. These communications, therefore, have become a major inconvenience. Because they no longer provide value, they now, for the most part, have become irritating.

We are now:

- irritated by the amount of direct mail that we receive;
- irritated by the number of spam e-mails that monopolize our inbox;
- irritated when we answer a cold call;
- irritated when we are interrupted by advertising when we are busy trying to do something else.

Because this kind of marketing works on repetition, continually e-mailing, continually cold calling or continually advertising, companies that still pursue this form of marketing are set to continually irritate their potential customers. Not, perhaps, the best way of communicating their message.

Any form of direct communication – for example e-mail, direct mail or telephone calls – that can be considered intrusive by a prospect and has not been requested, will damage your brand. In a world where customers have both the access to knowledge and the array of choices to make their decisions, at their convenience, these communications, far from being welcomed, are likely to be seen in an extremely negative light. Of course, there will always be exceptions to the rule. However, it is an extremely tenuous marketing strategy to spend valuable resources attempting to be one of the exceptions.

While it is possible that an advert may resonate with a prospect and over time lead to a sale, one has to question whether this model is the most efficient way of reaching potential customers. With the fragmentation of the media and subsequently the declining reach that any single piece of advertising has, we are moving towards a world where the return on investment does not make sense for all but the biggest brands and companies within their sector. When observing companies that still insist on shouting at their potential customers, I am reminded of something Robert Stephens[15] said: 'Advertising is a tax for having an unremarkable product.'

Consumers no longer use advertising in the way they once did: as a major resource for gaining knowledge regarding new products and services available in the market. Today, customers have all the access to information they need, at their time of choosing. Moreover, when advertising was used as an information source, it had a great influence on our thinking as it was a form of social proof. This is because we give a certain amount of credibility to sources providing us with new knowledge. In other words, we believed that the adverts reflected what our contemporaries thought.

Where customers now go for information

Today, as we have become more cynical, sophisticated and savvy, and live in a more connected world with mobile phones, text messaging, blogs, forums, wikis, instant messaging and social networks, we take more of our social proof directly from each other, thus reducing the influence that advertising once had. Word of mouth from our peers is now much more influential than any single piece of advertising. Think about it. If you want a new product or service today, there are probably only two places you will go: you will search on the web or you will ask your network.

By network, we are talking about family, friends, colleagues and connections in the online communities to which you belong. Between your network and the information available on the internet, you will probably have all the information required, regarding possible suppliers, to move your purchasing decision forward. It is unlikely that you will need to go anywhere else. This being the case, does it mean that the only marketing that matters now is online and word of mouth?

Both these forms of marketing put the customer firmly in control. It is up to people themselves whether they aid your word-of-mouth marketing by talking about you or referring you to others. Meanwhile, when prospects search online, they will browse and explore the sites and information of their choosing. In fact, the internet is the worst vehicle for finding a new customer. If you enter into the Google search bar 'I would like a new customer', nothing of value will be produced. The key to being successful online is for you to be where prospects look. At that juncture, you can communicate with them, providing resources and information of value, and, in this way, hope to start a worthwhile engagement.

Whether it is word of mouth by referral or online search, both these routes require your customer to come to you. This is in contrast to the old model of marketing where you shouted very loudly at prospects to grab their attention, hoping to gain a worthwhile response.

Today, customers have created barriers. They screen out the shouting because it no longer provides them with any value. With an abundance of choice and easy access to information via their networks and the internet, customers will find you at a time of their choosing. This being the case, is it not time we created a new marketing model to embrace the new world of technology and the internet?

KEY-POINT SUMMARY

● As technology and the internet play a greater part in our lives, we are seeing a shift in the dynamics of scarcity and abundance.

● In a world before the internet, consumers did not have easy access to information. Therefore, while companies would shout to sell their products and services, consumers were prepared to listen as these messages were often a valuable source of information.

● Consumers now have access to the information they require at their convenience. Consequently, receiving intrusive communications from companies, at the convenience of a business, has become increasingly irritating.

● As consumers live in a more connected world, with mobile phones, text messaging, blogs, forums, wikis, instant messaging, social networks etc, they take more of their social proof directly from each other. This reduces the influence that advertising once had.

● Most people today will rely on only two sources when looking to make a purchase: searching on the internet and asking their network. Both these channels of online and word of mouth rely on customers approaching your business at a time of their choosing.

Transactions to engagement

The shift from scarcity to abundance has huge implications for marketing. Ostensibly it means that the traditional model of marketing, and the way in which companies acquired new customers, is broken.

Previously, marketing operated as a funnel (Figure 3.1). It worked by companies paying a lot of money to 'shout' at their potential customers. The more money they had, the more often they tended to shout, via vehicles such as direct mail, cold calling, leaflet drops, advertising etc. Some people reacted to the shouting. That action was referred to as response. In business-to-consumer marketing, it was hoped that this response would result in a direct increase in sales. In business-to-business marketing this increase would come by following up the response, with prospects being qualified out, until eventually there were some paying customers at the end. Thus, a process that could have started with 20,000 direct mail shots might end with 20 paying customers; hence the funnel. As long as the income generated by the paying customers covered the cost of the campaign, with some left over for profit, a company would have made a return on investment and the marketing would be regarded as a success.

The funnel worked in a world of scarcity of choice and information. This model of marketing was completely transactional; it was a means to an end. It was all about the company selling its products and services. Businesses were concerned only, initially, with the response

FIGURE 3.1 Transactional marketing funnel

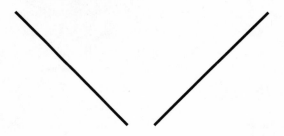

and ultimately with the transactions that their marketing generated. Customers put up with the shouting because it provided them with information to which they had no other access.

As we have seen, however, the web has now provided almost all the information a customer requires and at their convenience. Consequently, they are less tolerant of companies shouting at them in the way they once did.

Companies that still resort to using the funnel model create a mismatch between the way they market themselves and the way their customers look for a new supplier. Previously, customers had limited access to information and were also very restricted by locality. Consequently, a buyer would have easy access to only a handful of options. Therefore, continual shouting at a potential customer had some intrinsic value for a company. Statistically, at any one time, the majority of consumers would not be in the market for a particular product or service. However, because of the limited choice available, there was a very good chance that, when ready to buy, they would remember your shouting and subsequently, your company. As a result, over the long term, there was the potential for a business to achieve a healthy return on investment from its shouting. Companies would shout via advertising, direct mail, inserts in newspapers, telemarketing, trade press etc, but these were the very resources customers would use to acquire much of their information; hence, materials were often kept, to be referred to at a later date.

Today, this is simply not the case. Consumers are no longer limited by the handful of suppliers they had previously. In most areas of our lives we now have thousands of options. Most people access these alternatives in two ways: first, via their network, consisting of friends, family, colleagues, online connections and companies with which they are already engaged, or second, browsing the internet. Companies can shout frequently. However, it is far less likely today that this shouting will lead a customer to its door at the appropriate time. Sending out a direct mail will not generate a word-of-mouth referral and a business can send thousands of e-mails and still not be found when a potential customer is browsing the internet. The funnel was more about the supplier than it ever was about the customer. This approach does not work in a world where the customer has been empowered. Today, customers expect more from you than just being shouted at.

Interestingly enough, the exception that proves the rule is that of local takeaways, such as pizza, Chinese and curry. This is one of the rare occasions where we are extremely limited by locality, as most people are unwilling to drive too far to pick up a takeout. Because we know there are very few options available, most people are prepared to rely on the menus that are put through their doors, rather than going online to find something. Therefore, the menus still provide householders with value, as they are a reliable source of information and kept for when they become relevant. This is one of the uncommon examples where, at the moment, the shouting model is relatively well received. The question is whether even this is sustainable over the long term. My guess is that over time, there will be a move to digital, because of the convenience it will offer. For example, your local takeaway will be able to have your regular order stored on computer. By using your mobile, with one press of a button, it will be available for collection in 20 minutes.

The limitations of traditional 'relationship marketing'

The funnel model of marketing, which results in shouting at customers, is failing because it no longer provides any value for those it is targeting.

Creating more value was first addressed by Leonard Berry, who, in 1983, coined the term 'relationship marketing'.[1] Relationship marketing emphasized the role marketing played in not just acquiring clients, but retaining them over the long term. It recognized the enduring value of keeping customers and the significant impact it could make to a business's success. In fact, relationship marketing was not intended as a process for acquiring new customers at all. Rather, it was a mechanism for client retention. In other words, many of the businesses that advocate relationship marketing are still using transactional marketing and the traditional funnel to obtain new customers. Only once these customers are acquired is the relationship approach used to retain them.

The introduction of relationship marketing led to companies becoming increasingly concerned with providing good customer service. It also encouraged them to have a better understanding of their clients. This meant that companies took a more analytical approach to figuring out customer preferences and consequently targeted consumers with increasingly relevant messaging. This was aided by the advancement in computer technology, which made a more comprehensive database marketing approach viable. While many of these developments were positive, most companies' understanding of relationship marketing was unsatisfactory. Essentially, it amounted to companies continuing to shout at their database of clients, only this time the message was more targeted, and they used your first name. When analysed, the way most businesses implemented relationship marketing had little to do with developing any kind of relationship whatsoever.

Instead, as companies developed a greater knowledge of their customers, more targeted and personalized messages enabled businesses to upsell and extract more value from them. Most companies, however, contacted their customers only in order to sell them something. While a more efficient approach to upselling might have increased the number of customer transactions, this did not necessarily mean that a relationship was being developed. Essentially, for most businesses, what was called relationship marketing was ultimately a more sophisticated transactional approach to selling to a database of existing clients.

Moreover, acquiring a client through the transactional model of marketing makes the switch to a true relationship model difficult. This is because the company, inadvertently, has set the wrong tone for the relationship. After bombarding potential customers with a plethora of e-shots and mailers, it is no easy task to switch from the megaphone to the more intimate frame necessary to develop a relationship. The transactional approach to marketing, however it is dressed up, is about return on investment and getting customers to buy. Inherent in this is the implication that the deal is more important than anything else.

The mere fact that a business chooses to shout at its potential customers, despite the reality that most people find this increasingly obtrusive, speaks volumes about the company's regard for its potential patrons. A sudden switch from this, to the suggestion that the relationship is paramount and that as a company you care, is not perceived as genuine in the eyes of the customer. In other words, shouting at your clientele subsequently creates a barrier to developing any meaningful relationship; an impediment created by the company itself. In a world before the internet, where most businesses shouted and customers were not empowered, this less than authentic approach was accepted. Basically, people had no other expectation. However, with the plethora of choice and information at everybody's fingertips today, consumers see through this less than genuine approach by which many companies continue to address them.

Striving for 'relationships' is not enough

So, in reality, relationship marketing has been a more targeted, cleverer, transactional approach to existing customers. In a world of the internet and increased consumer empowerment, we need a more value-based model. However, most businesses have failed to do this. Many companies would acknowledge the requirement to give customers more value and strengthen relationships. Their lack of success in achieving this is because the term 'relationship' itself is unhelpful and misleading.

Allow me to explain. We all use a plethora of companies on a regular basis, with which we do not want a relationship. For example, I use Google for searching online, Tesco for shopping, MBNA for my credit card and O_2 for my mobile phone. Not a week goes by when I do not use the services of all these providers. However, I do not want a relationship with them, although they may want one with me. Being a regular user of these companies' services, I would imagine that, in marketing parlance, they would regard themselves as having a relationship with me. How do they measure that relationship? Is it when I make another transaction? Is it because I regularly use their product or service?

In our private lives, personal relationships are reciprocal; I like you and you like me. Over time, this evolves into a deep connectedness between two people. However, most companies' dealings with a customer are purely transactional. It just isn't the same. They give me something I want because I am paying for it. There is nothing more than that. As these companies learn more about me and my buying habits, I may be tempted with more relevant and enticing offers. This may mean that I spend more with them. This amounts to a sophisticated transactional approach, which is what relationship marketing has become. Having more data on me and therefore being able to deliver increasingly relevant messages does not constitute having a relationship.

For example, before switching to O_2 as my mobile provider, I had previously been with another company for a number of years. I used its service every day and spent a considerable amount of money with it. Occasionally I would call its customer service team with a problem or enquiry and every year I entered into a dialogue when it came to upgrading my phone and renewing my contract. To all intents and purposes, this company would have assumed that it had a relationship with me. However, having decided there were better offers to be had elsewhere, I left the company in one phone call. I never complained, or gave any indication that this was about to happen. After years of patronage, I ended our perceived relationship in under five minutes.

It is hard to imagine a scenario where, after years of friendship with another human being, you would be prepared to end that relationship in a five-minute phone call, without any prior warning or indication that the relationship was in trouble. Personal relationships are not transactional in nature. They are entered into voluntarily by both sides and we generally place a great value on them. In my example with the mobile provider, this was simply not the case. The relationship was transactional. I was paying for the service that I received. Therefore, when I decided I could get better value elsewhere, I felt no obligation to my previous supplier. Having always paid for the service, I felt no duty of care. This being the case, in business, the term 'relationship' is an unhelpful gauge for strategically understanding your company's position with its customers.

Understand, I am not suggesting that relationships in business do not matter. On the contrary, one-to-one interactions with customers take place in many companies. Whether you are a business owner, salesperson, customer service representative, receptionist, account manager or anyone else, it is important that you develop good relations with clients and prospects. The old adage, 'people buy people', is true. Therefore, it makes sense that any person who interacts with customers should be personable and provide their client with a pleasurable experience. Repeated contacts with an individual can lead to a relationship developing which will add value to a customer. In turn, this will increase the likelihood of them spending more and staying with the business.

Not all companies have the opportunity to have a personal dialogue with their clients. Where applicable, these personal relationships are extremely important. When a company knows that these interactions take place, it should ensure that its staff are well trained and have the ability to handle these interactions effectively. These personal relationships become part of the way a company interacts with its customers. It is part of their strategy. **However, these relationships do not define the strategy.**

'Relationship' is a very passive word. Ultimately, all it means is being connected. Of course, every business is connected with every customer by the mere fact that they have bought something. The word 'relationship', though, is not helpful in defining a strategy for retaining customers. Being connected is not enough. Companies need a gauge for being able to measure just how connected they are. Relationships are the wrong measure for this. On the one hand, it is too passive a term. Being connected, in itself, is meaningless. On the other hand, it is inappropriate. With few exceptions, customers are not looking for the type of connectedness they obtain through personal relationships with friends and family. What we require is a term that measures connectedness based on value, which is the very basis for any interaction that takes place between company and client. Judging this by 'relationship' is not the right criterion.

Moreover, relationship marketing is not, and never has been, a strategy for acquiring customers at all. The world has moved on. Customers have more choice and access to information than ever before. Businesses have unprecedented technology, giving them the wherewithal to deliver better value to prospects and customers than they had previously. Today, in order to acquire new customers, companies need to leave the traditional funnel mode of marketing behind. Companies need a framework more robust than relationship marketing for understanding the value they provide in order to retain their customers.

Introducing 'customer engagement' marketing

The model that answers these challenges is customer engagement. 'To engage' means to keep busy. Engagement implies that I am occupying my prospect or customer. Of course, they will participate only if they perceive they are receiving value. Thus, customer engagement is reciprocal. By providing value to prospects and customers they, in turn, respond by giving of their time. This is an effective measure, because it means that a company is appraising the exact criterion which a consumer subconsciously uses to decide whether to interact with that business.

In order for customer engagement to be an effective strategy, companies must have a clear understanding of what we mean by the term 'value': value is simply when the cost of having or doing something is *less* than the cost of not having or doing it. In other words, I am better off spending my time or money doing this than not doing it because, by not doing it, I am missing out and consequently putting myself in a worse situation.

For example, I will deem it worthwhile spending two dollars on an ice cream if I perceive that, at that moment, my life would be worse off if I did not have the ice cream and I kept the two dollars. Similarly, a business may see value in spending $50,000 on a new IT infrastructure because without this spend it may fear that it will be unable to compete within its market and, therefore, be worse off. In customer engagement terms, value can be ascertained with one simple question: 'If I were my customer, would I give up my time for this?'

Customer engagement involves finding value for your prospects and clients around the product or service that you provide. Today, simply concentrating your marketing on the product or service you offer is not enough. For example, if you run a recruitment company, simply talking about the services you offer will be of interest only to those people who currently require new members of staff. Your marketing, therefore, will have relevance only to those looking for a candidate now, which is exactly what happened in the transactional model of marketing. Everyone else would screen the message out as irrelevant.

Alternatively, by understanding the value you can provide, which relates to your product or service, you can widen your appeal and engage with those potential customers who currently have no interest in your actual product or service. So, for example, the recruitment company might produce tip sheets on subjects such as 'how to ensure you retain your best members of staff' or '10 ideas for improving staff morale'. These tip sheets would not be designed to promote their brand but be of generic value to any company with employees.

Relationship marketing became a more sophisticated transactional approach because communications tended to relate directly to a purchase. Customer engagement is not based on an immediate transaction – it is purely value led. By offering potential customers and clients something worthwhile, on a frequent basis, a business builds trust and credibility with its audience. When a customer is ready to buy, it is likely that, at the very least, you will be one of the businesses to which they look as a potential supplier. Having had the opportunity to demonstrate your expertise and give value to a prospect, they may very well be predisposed to want to use you.

From 'return on investment' to 'return on engagement'

In the technological world, one of the scarcest resources available is customer attention. The demands of modern life, with e-mails, texts, phone calls, social networks, 24-hour news, a multitude of television channels and a plethora of websites all available at any place and any time, mean that getting customers to take notice of you is extremely difficult. Of course, this means that it is equally challenging for everyone else, including your competitors. Once you have your customers' and potential customers' attention, you are much more likely to win their business at the appropriate time. The battle in the marketplace is no longer for transactions. Rather, it is for attention. Quite simply, those companies with customer attention win. Therefore, we need to replace the old model of marketing, which was measured by ROI (return on investment), with a new model based on ROE (return on engagement). For, if you are engaging with your audience, it means that you have their attention and, ultimately, this will lead to business growth.

The customer engagement model of marketing is a complete reversal of the traditional funnel. In fact, we turn the funnel 180 degrees so that it is completely on its head. What you are left with is the narrow spout at the top with the wide base at the bottom (Figure 3.2).

The narrow spout represents where prospects start engaging with us. We are no longer going to shout at them, for example by sending out 100,000 e-mails. Instead, they are going to come to us. It is far more likely that prospects will come to us; one, five, or ten at a time. It is extremely unlikely that we will be approached by 100,000 people at once. Therefore, the spout at the top is very narrow, representing the far fewer prospects with whom we begin to engage at any one time. Once a prospect has, metaphorically, raised their hand and indicated that they would like to engage with us, they drop through the narrow

FIGURE 3.2 Engagement marketing funnel

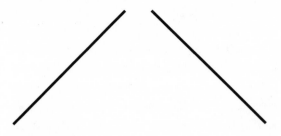

spout into the wider base. In an ideal world, this base continues to grow wider and wider.

The reason the wide base is forever expanding is because, unlike the traditional funnel, we are not interested in qualifying anybody out. The scarcest resource for businesses today is customer attention. Those companies with the attention of their potential customers win. Therefore, the more attention we have, the better it is. Marketing today requires us to keep as many people engaged as possible.

Firstly, the more people we have engaged, the more customers we will eventually acquire. For example, if over time you ascertain that, statistically, 15 per cent of your engaged audience buy, then, of course, 15 per cent of 100 engaged prospects is a lot fewer than 15 per cent of 1,000. Secondly, people will engage with your business only if they are receiving value. Even if they do not become paying customers, some of these prospects will tell others about your company. Although many of your engaged audience will not be customers, some of them will be responsible for attracting new prospects and, therefore, delivering new customers and growing your business.

The cost of engagement before the ubiquity of modern technology would have been prohibitively high. Attempting to give value and stay in contact with potentially thousands of people would have been beyond what most companies could sensibly afford. Concentrating on transactions was the only option open to most businesses. However, utilizing all aspects of modern communications, distribution and advanced customer relationship management tools means that even the smallest business can engage with potentially millions of prospects at negligible cost.

In fact, not only does the customer engagement model of marketing not require prospects to be qualified out of the funnel, but ideally, no prospect or customer would ever leave. Thus, the base would become increasingly wide. Of course, there will be natural attrition. In a business-to-consumer scenario, customers move away and disappear. In business-to-business, companies merge, are bought out and go bust. However, aside from this natural attrition, ideally a business will give enough ongoing value to keep all its prospects engaged.

This can be monitored. For example, website analytics packages can be used in order to track who visits your website, where they come from, what they look at and for how long etc. Meanwhile, services that monitor and alert you to online conversations involving your business, and your market, will allow you to track the reactions your company receives to the activities it undertakes. It will also allow your business to respond to the comments being made. In addition, customer relationship management software enables you to keep a detailed history of any interactions made directly with a customer. In so doing, you will gain insights as to how you will be able to offer and provide further value in the future.

If a company identifies that there is a certain point in their journey when people leave, then it would be required to do everything it can to prevent this from happening in the future. By asking consumers, a company should be able to realize why it is no longer able to provide value at this juncture, and then do its best to rectify this situation.

Engaging on your customer's terms

There is a myriad of platforms available with which to engage customers. Some may choose to access content from your website or blog, while others may choose to subscribe to e-mail newsletters or RSS feeds (Really Simple Syndication)[2] of your content. Meanwhile, others may choose to follow you on Twitter, enter into dialogue on a LinkedIn forum or industry website, or connect with you via Facebook or another network. The key is to identify the places that your prospects and customers like to visit and be available in those places. This could be a particular industry forum or a popular social network. Offline, this could translate into being present at the major industry event or belonging to a particular association. The point is that customers and prospects want to interact on their terms. By making yourself available on all the different platforms that your various customers and prospects enjoy using, you will make it easy to engage. Wherever they are is where you should be. If you offer the path of least resistance, it is much more likely that they will choose to take it.

A company may host offline seminars or online webinars. Alternatively, it may produce white papers, tip sheets or 'how to' articles. It may write powerful think pieces, create games, hold competitions or any number of alternatives. It is up to individual businesses to ascertain what combination of options will be of most value to their audience. Similarly, they will decide how often new ideas and material will need to be created in order to keep their public interested, while at the same time not overloading them.

The key to making engagement work, as a marketing strategy, is to listen intently to the conversations your prospects and customers are having online and in the forums and networks in which they participate. In so doing, you will gain an understanding of your prospects and customers. When this is combined with what they tell you directly, it will enable you to ensure that all your communication is value led.

In this way, over time, your audience will be encouraged to sign up on your website, register on your blog, connect with you on Facebook or LinkedIn or follow you on Twitter. Engagement can work only if, over the long term, people reveal themselves to you. The more you can learn about your customers and prospects, both anecdotally and by asking questions, the more value you can deliver. Good data capture is essential. Without the ability to understand customer behaviour, likes and dislikes, and preferences, it will be extremely difficult to provide value on an ongoing basis.

Data capture is a long-term strategy. An attempt to ask customers for too many personal details when they have just discovered that you exist is likely to deter them. Rather, you can attempt to get a greater understanding of your customers and prospects gradually and over a long period of time. For example, if a visitor to your website is encouraged to sign up to receive a white paper and you ask them too many questions, they may very well not bother. Instead, on initial sign-up, you may simply require a name and e-mail address. Several months later, they may be interested in a variety of webinars. It could be that at this juncture it is relevant to ask them for a company name and the market sector in which they operate. If your business subsequently chooses to run some offline activities it would then be reasonable to ask them for a geographical location in order to inform them of when you will be in their area. You can see that, over time, an enormous amount of data can potentially be collected, but this should not be attempted all in one go and on the first point of contact.

Similarly, customer behaviour can also be monitored. If certain pages of your website are never visited or are looked at infrequently and for a short period of time, it is possible that they are failing to give value and should be replaced. If a high proportion of your customers and engaged prospects regularly watch your videos but do not access many of your articles, it may be an indicator of the way in which they like you to communicate. The more knowledge and understanding you gather, the more relevant you can be and the increased value you can give. Thus, a virtuous circle is developed.

Becoming a trusted source of information

Giving value and engaging with prospects will eventually lead to business in a world of increased choice. Previously, when people were limited by the number of suppliers available, they would often see most or even all of them. In other words, if there were three major suppliers in my area for a particular service, it would make sense to see all three and then make a purchasing decision. Today, with very little effort, searching online can often uncover tens, hundreds or even thousands of suppliers when looking for a new service. The challenge is not finding what we want, but making sense of the inordinate amount of choice that we face. This is coupled with the fact that most of us are extremely time poor. In short, we rarely have the time to research extensively and educate ourselves about any particular market. In these circumstances, we rely on trusted sources of information.

If you are engaged with a potential customer and providing them with value on a regular basis, you will have already built a certain amount of credibility with them. Over time, you become one of their trusted sources of information. When looking for a particular product or service that you supply, it is very likely that your engaged prospect will be predisposed to using you. In some cases, they may not even look elsewhere. In other cases, they may consider a few alternatives to benchmark what you provide. However, having regular engagement increases your chances of winning their business. Of course, this does not guarantee that you will obtain the order in every situation. However, by engaging with your prospects, giving them value and therefore winning their attention, you put yourself in an excellent position to acquire their business at the relevant time.

In a world of so much choice, the other source of reliable information is often our personal network – our friends, family, colleagues and online connections. When looking for a new supplier, we will often ask for our network's recommendations. These referrals come from trusted sources. Coupled with the fact that we are short of time, we are often predisposed to giving the business to those companies to whom we are referred. If they come across well and meet our expectations, we are very likely to use them. Word-of-mouth referrals are an extremely important source of new business. The more people we engage with, the more people will know about us. Some of those with whom we have built credibility and trust will provide us with referrals over time.

Finally, the more people with whom we engage, the more we will be talked about. It also increases the likelihood of content and materials that we create being shared. Online, these conversations and links to content make us easier to find in the search engines. Engagement marketing aligns with the major ways that buyers look for, and source, new providers. Whether they are searching online, asking their networks or depending on reliable sources of information, in order to make sense of the plethora of choices available, engagement marketing will raise the possibility that your business receives these enquiries.

The transactional funnel model of marketing was based on shouting very loudly in order to find clients to buy your wares. In this model, marketing was a means to an end. Return on investment was measured. It was purchases that counted.

The customer engagement model focuses on giving value around the product or services you deliver. This value is not tied to any purchase, but is interesting to your audience in its own right. In this way, you become 'sticky' or attractive. By doing this on an ongoing basis, customers and prospects will keep wanting to interact with you. 'Sticky marketing', therefore, is a fundamental underlying principle of customer engagement.

In this model, marketing is not a means to an end; it is an end in itself. Value encourages people to interact with your business on a regular basis. Consequently, you will have their attention, a scarce resource but vital to a business. The new measurement is ROE (return on engagement). As long as your business is engaging with an increasing number of prospects and customers, this hard-won attention will result in your company thriving.

KEY-POINT SUMMARY

- Customer engagement marketing requires prospects and customers to participate. By providing them with value, they will respond by giving of their time. Value can be ascertained with one simple question: 'If I were my customer, would I give up my time for this?'

- Value is created around the product or services that you provide. Today, merely concentrating your marketing on the product or service itself is not enough.

- The new marketing model is based on 'return on engagement'. If you are engaging with prospects and customers, it means that you have their attention. The new battle in marketing today is for customer attention.

- Unlike in the traditional funnel, the new model of marketing is inclusive. We do not wish to qualify anybody out. Many engaged prospects will contribute to word-of-mouth recommendations and, online, may contribute to helping us to be found through links, mentions etc.

- A good customer relationship management tool, a website analytics package and monitoring online conversations are essential in enhancing your understanding of customers and prospects alike. This, in turn, will enable you to add value and engage with your clientele.

- One key to successful engagement is to identify the places that your prospects and customers like to visit, for example particular industry blogs, industry forums, social networks, events and industry associations. Having done this, you should have a presence in these places.

- The plethora of choice that consumers face means that we all rely on trusted sources of information which we use as filters. By regularly engaging with your clientele and providing them with value, over time, you become one of those trusted sources.

PART 03

DEVELOPING AN EFFECTIVE MARKETING STRATEGY

CHAPTER 04

Benefits to problems

In 1961, at his inaugural address, President John F Kennedy famously said 'Ask not what your country can do for you, but what you can do for your country.'[1] This sentiment could be used to describe what marketing should be delivering today: 'Ask not what your Marketing can do for you, but what your Marketing can do for your customer.'

Becoming 'sticky', and adopting the customer engagement model of marketing, ie turning the funnel upside down, requires a change in approach from other traditional marketing conventions. Among these is the way in which messages are produced. Marketers have routinely focused on conveying the benefits of their product or service to potential buyers. This type of messaging is, by definition, transactional in nature.

Benefits are benefits only when you are ready to buy. For example, a human resources consultancy may communicate an array of benefits in using its service. It may emphasize the protection it can provide for your business against litigation, therefore keeping your business safe. It could stress its ability to make sure your company is compliant with current rules and regulations, mitigating the chances of receiving fines or facing other difficulties. Finally, it could articulate the work it undertakes in establishing efficient practices, saving both time and money. However, if you are not currently in the market for any HR service, or already have a supplier, these benefits are likely to be of little interest. In order to become 'sticky' and engage prospects and customers, you have to stop focusing on transactions and find value around the product or service you deliver.

Your product or service itself will only be of interest at the point someone is looking to buy. Moreover, once they have bought, information about what you do will have little relevance until such time as they are looking to make another purchase. In order to have dialogue both before a purchase is considered and subsequently after it has been made, the focus must be on the value surrounding your offering, rather than the offering itself. On this, benefit messaging completely fails.

An example of transactional marketing

For example, an owner of a car dealership offers to host a Chamber of Commerce event as a gesture of goodwill to the local business community. This, in itself, is a good example of engagement marketing. The owner provides great value for provincial companies by facilitating the hosting of an exciting event in their area. This action assists in beginning to establish a degree of credibility and trust. Meanwhile, an offshoot is that more people will have the opportunity to become familiar with the existence and location of the showroom as well as see some of the products close up.

The head of the Chamber of Commerce asks the dealer, as the host, to welcome everybody and at the same time take the opportunity to say a few words about the showroom. Unfortunately, at this juncture, our dealer resorts to more traditional marketing conventions by introducing the audience to an attractive PowerPoint slide of the latest family saloon. During the welcome, the dealer spends just a few minutes speaking about the benefits of the car.

Our dealer presents the fact that it is the most fuel-efficient car in its class, which means that it is inexpensive to run and leaves more money in your pocket, and that it has the lowest emissions of any car currently on the market, which means that you can have a beautiful new saloon and still be adhering to environmental recommendations. The dealer proudly states that it has been voted the safest saloon in all the European tests, which means that it is the best car available in which to keep your family safe.

By concentrating on the benefits of the new car, the presentation is customer focused in that it relates to why the car will improve a customer's driving situation. However, it is also a transactionally focused presentation. It is all about why the car would make a good purchase. Benefits are benefits only when I am ready to buy. If I am sitting in the audience and am currently not looking for a new car, the presentation is irrelevant and, therefore, boring. As, statistically, most people will not currently be in the market for a new car, then isn't the welcome a waste of time?

It is highly likely that most of the audience will go home and simply forget about the presentation. This is a missed opportunity in a world where customer attention is so precious. It is possible, though, that the presentation may actually have had a detrimental effect. Forcing visitors to listen to irrelevant sales messages may result in the loss of some of the goodwill obtained by providing the car showroom to the Chamber in the first place.

The success of our dealer's speech relies solely on timing, ie someone in the room currently looking for a new car. Unless an individual makes an enquiry, very little will have been gained from the event. Knowing this, our dealer, a really good transactional marketer, also decides to hold a prize draw. On entering the venue, patrons are encouraged to place their business cards in a hat for the chance to win a bottle of champagne, thus allowing the car showroom to collect personal details of the attendees. This enables the dealer to follow up an unsuccessful presentation with a variety of spam e-mails. Anyone who left the showroom either apathetic or even with some goodwill is likely to be left disgruntled on receipt of repetitive, unwanted e-mails. This campaign is an example of transactional marketing. That is, shout at people about the benefits of your products and hope that someone buys. If a purchase was made as a result of this campaign, it would probably be deemed a success. Little consideration would be given to everybody else who is likely to have been left with a slightly sour taste in their mouths.

The alternative approach: providing value around your product or service

The customer engagement model of marketing would take a completely different approach. The focus would be on providing value for the customer rather than any short-term transaction. This cannot be done by concentrating on benefits, which, by definition, are about the product or service you sell.

Instead, this time our car dealer would think about the challenges and issues that all car drivers face. For example, they are confronted by increasingly high insurance premiums. They worry about road safety, especially those drivers who are transporting younger members of their family. Compliance and changing regulations, such as the laws regarding mobile phone use, provide other questions that need to be answered. Finally, the running of the vehicle and car maintenance matters, eg how to achieve the best fuel consumption and maximizing the wear on your tyres are perennial concerns.

All of these subjects could provide our car dealer with valuable material for a short presentation. He or she could talk about factors that will help reduce your car insurance, or five top tips, unknown to most drivers, that would make them safer on the road. Alternatively, the dealer could chat about new regulations and mistakes people inadvertently make, which are actually against the law, or could decide, instead, to convey expert recommendations in obtaining the optimum performance from your car.

No matter what subject our car dealer chooses to cover during the two- or three-minute welcome, the nature of the presentation changes completely. By giving information that is useful to all drivers, the audience gains value and is, therefore, more likely to regard the car brand and showroom in a favourable light. The car dealer, by presenting this material, demonstrates the firm's knowledge in its field, which, in turn, helps to build trust. In so doing, it increases the likelihood that next time a member of this Chamber of Commerce requires advice about a car, they will visit this showroom.

Moreover, by providing the audience with value, our car dealer can offer as a follow-up something more substantial than a bottle of champagne and spam e-mails. By creating a tip sheet and announcing its availability on the firm's website, our dealer gives members of the audience a reason to engage further. In fact, our car dealer could produce other tip sheets on different subjects, which can also be downloaded from the site. Those attendees who provide their e-mail address in order to receive the download would have initiated the beginnings of customer engagement. Not only is it possible that some people may choose to share these tip sheets with others, but they can also be used as mini articles that can be placed on other websites and in magazines with links back to the showroom's own website. The presentation could even be recorded and posted on a platform like YouTube, eg 'The best way to improve your vehicle's fuel consumption'. Dealing with universal problems that drivers face gives the material wide appeal, making it more likely that it will be watched and shared.

Thus, a short presentation can be the catalyst for starting valuable customer engagement with a number of members of the audience, as well as providing an array of other opportunities to use the material. By imparting good information and providing consistent value, our car dealer's content will be used and shared, and its base of engaged customers will grow. As this engagement develops, it will become a trusted source and filter of information about 'all things cars' for this particular group of people. Over time, some of these people will buy from the dealer, while others may refer this particular showroom to individuals in their network. However, a presentation with this result could never be created by concentrating on benefits.

The shortcomings of benefit messaging

Benefits will not help you understand the value around what you do or provide an insight into the universal issues that your customer experiences. Benefits merely focus on the transaction, dispensing reasons as to why a customer should buy a particular product or service. Thinking in terms of benefits will not assist you in looking at the wider concerns of a prospect and, therefore, being able to take a more holistic approach. A focus on benefits will not help a business establish a customer engagement approach to their marketing. Our car dealer's successful presentation was arrived at by understanding the challenges and problems that the audience faced. Benefits are benefits only when I am ready to buy. Challenges and problems are more universal. For example:

- I may not be in the market for a car right now, but I would like to achieve better fuel consumption with my current vehicle.
- I may not want to buy a brand new suit today, but I would like to know how to make the best of my existing wardrobe.
- I may not be looking to change my accountant, but I am interested in benchmarking their performance and seeing if I am paying too much tax.

Not only does a problem approach allow you to understand the value around your product or service, it more accurately reflects the way in which people search online. Today, more people browse the internet looking for content and information than anything else.[2] Many people will have particular preferences for websites they use to catch up on news or use for entertainment. However, when people search online, looking for something new, it is more often than not that they have a problem in mind. For example:

- I may search cinema listings: Issue? Where am I going on Friday night?
- I may search for the weather: Issue? What am I going to wear tomorrow?
- I may search on traffic reports: Issue? What time do I need to leave my house in order to arrive at my meeting on time?

So, for example, someone could be searching the internet for local accountants. There may be a variety of issues on their mind. It could be that they feel dissatisfied with the current service they are receiving and want to know what else is available. Alternatively, they may be unhappy with the level of tax they are paying. Of course, it could also be that they are looking for an accountant for the first time and are researching to learn about the possible options. Landing on a home page that details the benefits of a particular firm is unlikely to resonate with a potential client. For example, typical messages may focus on:

- the personal and friendly service this particular firm provides;
- its aim to save you money on your tax bill;
- the formidable range of expertise and experience it can provide.

These messages, however, are merely platitudes. No accountancy firm is likely to claim that it provides an unfriendly service, doesn't wish to save you any money or has no experience or expertise to offer its clients. Therefore, these messages are bland and meaningless. Moreover, it is unlikely that the primary aim of any search is to find the friendliest accountant or the one that makes the most outlandish claims with regard to how much money it may be able to save.

Ask the right question

A far better approach, therefore, is to focus on the issues a potential client is likely to have when initiating their search. So, for example, a home page may ask three pertinent questions, with links the user can click to find the answers:

- Are you receiving a good service from your accountant? Click here for the 10 top deliverables that all accountants should provide.
- Are you paying too much tax? Answer our online questionnaire for an immediate idea as to whether you might be overpaying.
- Looking for a new accountant? Here are the five questions you should be asking every potential supplier.

It is far more likely that this approach will engage a new visitor to the site. It does not provide platitudes or meaningless promises, in which a customer is not interested. Rather, the content aligns itself with the type of questions a prospect is likely to be asking themselves. Of course, by talking with clients and using web analytics, which will provide details of the links visitors click on and the ones they ignore, you can constantly strive to perfect the messaging on your website. The principle, however, is sound. By thinking about the problems that your customers face, it is far more likely that your communications, whether online or offline, will align with any potential buyer's thought processes. In so doing, it will be much easier to engage with that prospect.

It is only by thinking in terms of problems that you will understand the wider value you can provide for a customer, built around what you do, rather than focusing on the product or service itself. It is this added value, not based on transactions, that will engage potential customers and enable you to build an ever-widening group of people who regularly interact with your business. This will allow you to turn the funnel on its head, engaging with a growing number of people, some of whom will share your content and refer you to others. Moreover, when they are ready to buy, it is more likely that, at the very least, you will receive an enquiry. The irony is that in a world where there is an abundance of choice, it is impossible to research all the options available. In this scenario, time pressure often means that, on many occasions, people do not exercise their choice at all. Therefore, if you have built up credibility and trust with a customer with whom you are regularly engaged, there is a very good chance that when they are ready to buy, you will receive the sale.

Problem Maps®

This being the case, a mechanism is required for being able to identify the issues that you solve for a customer and the value that can be created around these challenges. This can then be used as the basis of your customer engagement model. So let me introduce you to Problem Maps®.[3]

Problem Maps® are exactly this: they are a way of being able to understand the issues that start to lead a customer towards a purchase. They will also enable you to understand the value around your product or service in order to then come up with ideas and messages that will work within the customer engagement model. So let me explain how a Problem Map® works.

First, you need to draw a 16-box matrix as seen in Table 4.1. Alternatively, these can be downloaded from our website, stickymarketing.com.

TABLE 4.1 Problem Map® template

	Headline problem #1	Headline problem #2	Headline problem #3	Headline problem #4
Headline problem				
Resulting problem 'A'				
Resulting problem 'B'				
Resulting problem 'C'				

You start filling out a Problem Map® by considering four headline problems your potential customers may have, which you know you can solve. This is not about you, it is an exercise focused solely on your customer. It forces you to put yourself in your customer's shoes. These headline problems are issues that perennially challenge many typical prospects and customers. All four headline problems must be different.

Once you have entered these four headlines, you then need to identify three issues that result from each of the initial headlines. In every vertical column, the three resulting problems under each headline must also be different. In other words, once completed, each vertical column will contain four unique issues. However, resulting problems may be repeated under different headlines in other vertical columns. Therefore, although there are 16 boxes in your Problem Map® grid, you will have fewer unique problems. As a guide, a typical Problem Map® will contain 10–13 unique issues.

Table 4.2 is an example of a Problem Map® for a company we will name Jellybox Call Answering Service, a company providing call-answering services for businesses.

You can see that we have the four headline problems across the top, which are all different, and then underneath we have the three resulting problems. In every vertical column all four problems are different. However, in the horizontal 'Resulting Problem' columns, there is some overlap. So although, potentially, there could be 16 unique issues, in this case there are only 14.

When you are preparing a Problem Map® it is important not to be lazy and merely repeat the same resulting issues in various columns, because the result will be only seven or eight unique issues. On the other hand, you should expect there to be some overlap. Inevitably these problems are going to be connected, and that should result in some repetition.

TABLE 4.2 Jellybox Problem Map®

	Headline problem #1	Headline problem #2	Headline problem #3	Headline problem #4
Headline problem	I sometimes miss calls because we are a small company and not always available.	I am spending more money on receptionists than I would like.	I need my calls screened, but cannot afford a PA.	I struggle to deal with peaks and troughs in my business.
Resulting problem 'A'	People get the answerphone, which makes us look amateur.	I end up wasting company resources on staff I don't need.	I end up wasting valuable time on calls I shouldn't take.	I end up wasting company resources on staff I don't need.
Resulting problem 'B'	Opportunities go missing, because some people do not like leaving a message.	Less money to divert into other areas of the business.	I miss important calls, which annoys my customers.	Sometimes we miss opportunities because we are unable to cope with the call volume.
Resulting problem 'C'	I struggle to manage my time properly in the day as I am often distracted.	Carry a bigger overhead, so it is harder to be more competitive in the market.	I struggle to manage my time properly in the day as I am often distracted.	It affects other areas of the business, as members of staff are diverted away from important tasks.

Looking at the Problem Map®, there are certain key areas we can identify where Jellybox add value:

- It is a solution for small businesses to maintain a professional image and to better manage their time.
- It is a solution for bigger companies to save money, manage their resources more effectively and therefore become more competitive.
- It is a way for any company to be able to manage the dynamics of their business cycle.

Competing with bigger companies, managing time better, saving money, becoming more competitive and managing the dynamics of the business cycle are perennial issues that many people are concerned about all the time, not just if they are in the market for call-answering services.

The Problem Map® presents all sorts of opportunities for Jellybox to start engaging with companies within its target market areas. For example, it can produce a series of tip sheets, podcasts, videos and articles called 'How to present your small company in the right way'. By partnering with other providers of services it could produce some really engaging material which many small business websites, publications and associations would be happy to promote and distribute to their own members because it would add value. In turn, all of this may encourage people to engage with Jellybox and visit its website in order to receive other valuable material. It is even possible that some prospects will consider using a call-answering service, even though it had not previously occurred to them.

Using other providers and partnering with them, it can organize a seminar or a webinar online, aimed at finance directors and procurement departments, providing many ways of cutting costs off the bottom line. It could also partner with relevant associations and industry bodies who would invite their members to participate in this webinar or seminar. Therefore, no shouting needs to take place in order to get attendees there and give value.

Jellybox could employ a market research firm to do some investigation into how businesses, in certain industries that are seasonal etc, cope with the peaks and troughs of the business cycle. It would uncover the challenges they have and the solutions they employ. Relevant research like this can often create a story which leads to successful PR and articles being written for various publications. This is because independent research such as this carries credibility. This research would then be available for download on the Jellybox website, another way for initiating customer engagement.

Once you have a Problem Map®, you can really understand the value you can deliver around your product or service, and use this as the start of your customer engagement strategy. The key is always to put the customer first and make sure you are relevant and providing value.

Using Problem Maps® as the basis for engagement

Using Problem Maps® provides you with a mechanism for understanding your product or service through the eyes of a customer. This insight then enables a business to create value around its core offering, with which to engage prospects and customers alike. We can demonstrate this in the case of a neighbourhood burger bar, which we will call Benny's Burgers.

CASE STUDY   Example case study

Let's set the scene; Benny's Burgers is an independent burger bar run by a husband and wife team. Their vision is to produce burgers and chips, offering fast food but in a very healthy way, using fresh organic meat, fresh salads etc, the idea being that parents can feel good about taking their children there. They open up in a local market and start their marketing by leafleting the area. Their messaging is entirely 'benefit' led:

- Fresh organic meat – you get a healthy meal that tastes great!

- Variety menus – three-course meals that don't break the bank!

- A large car park and easy access – so it is a stress-free experience!

Now of course, unless I am in the market for burger and chips at that very moment, this messaging – in my day-to-day life – is probably not that relevant. It is very transactionally based. Shouting about their new restaurant does not get them very far. People don't come and they become disillusioned when customers fail to appear. It is time for Benny's Burgers to take a customer engagement approach by turning the funnel on its head. This process necessarily starts with a Problem Map®.

Marketing solutions to the problems

Looking at the Problem Map® in Table 4.3, it becomes clear that Benny's Burgers is a children's brand. Most of the problems involve feeding, occupying or marking special occasions with the kids. However, Benny's Burgers is unknown. It is also not the only brand in its area that provides activity displacement for children or ways to mark special occasions for the family. So how can it give value and engage its customers? One possible way is by leveraging partnerships.

It is springtime. Benny's Burgers draws a 20-mile radius from its restaurant and investigates all of the activity displacement provision for children in its area. It approaches all of the providers and proposes to promote their activities to its own customers if the right special offers can be agreed. Having decided on promotions with 10 particular companies, Benny's Burgers produces an attractive flyer entitled '10 things to do with your kids this summer', which focuses on the particular area in which it is based. This flyer contains offers which can be redeemed by way of coupons. For example: visit the zoo and a second child gets in free, one free regular popcorn when you visit the cinema for a children's matinee, £10 off a family ticket for the theme park on Mondays and Tuesdays etc. This flyer is then posted on its website and optimized in order to be found by the online search engines. This is achieved by using key words based around children's activities in its local area.

Benny's Burgers also successfully obtains coverage in the local paper. Each week of the summer holidays, the paper prints one coupon with a small feature related to the particular activity. At the bottom of each article it mentions that more offers like this can be downloaded from Benny's Burgers' website. Also, some of the companies with whom Benny's Burgers partners are happy to carry links on their website to Benny's Burgers' website, as are some local interest and community sites.

In order for parents to be able to cut out the coupons and use them at the appropriate destinations, they are requested simply to provide a name and e-mail address whereby the flyer is sent to them via e-mail. While the 10 offers have nothing to do with Benny's Burgers, there is a bonus, no 11, which provides special discounts at Benny's Burgers' restaurant. This promotion leads to numerous downloads of the flyer. Word of mouth is also generated as parents start to tell others about the availability of the coupons. The owners of Benny's Burgers start to see new customers visiting their restaurant and redeeming some of the vouchers.

This campaign benefits Benny's Burgers in a number of ways. It starts to position itself as a leading children's brand in its local area, generating a lot of goodwill with customers because of the enormous value it is imparting. By being associated with more established brands in its locality, it starts to gain credibility and trust, far exceeding what a new restaurant in its area would expect. The campaign attracts customers and engages many people. However, this is not about burgers and chips. This is about understanding the problems that its customers face and engaging customers by providing them with value associated with these issues.

Creating value

This example sees the funnel model being turned upside down. Benny's Burgers shouted at no one. Instead it has become attractive by creating value within a niche market and being discovered through search engines, the local paper and by word of mouth. As more people download the offers, thereby engaging with Benny's Burgers, its funnel becomes wider and wider.

By the end of the summer, Benny's Burgers has developed a large permission-based e-mail list. At this juncture, many companies would be tempted to send out regular special offers for the burger bar. This, however, would be a step back into the old world of transactional marketing. Messages relaying special offers are of no value unless you want to purchase a burger and chips at that moment. Moreover, however attractive the offers, regular receipt could become tiresome to even the most loyal of customers. Instead, Benny's Burgers continues with the customer engagement model. It commissions a designer to put together a series of mini activity booklets containing puzzles, quizzes, colouring, word searches and other exercises for children. During the winter, when the weekend weather report is bad, Benny's Burgers e-mails its booklet for parents to print off and be able to spend some time with their children. Although each activity booklet does contain a coupon with an offer for Benny's Burgers, that is not the focus of the communication. It is not about promoting burgers and chips, but providing value for the client.

These booklets are not just found on Benny's Burgers' website, but are also placed on some local community sites. As parents mention these booklets to others in conversation, and as children see them at friends' houses, some word of mouth is also created. The upside-down funnel continues to get wider. Benny's Burgers keeps its customers engaged and attracts new ones by focusing on providing value.

It is establishing itself as a major children's brand in its area and its restaurant is becoming busier. Its marketing, however, is not a means to an end, a way of just selling more product. By creating value, it engages customers, but the special coupons and activity booklets can be used without any purchase ever taking place. In other words, the marketing is an end in itself. It creates its own value. It is no longer about burgers and chips, or alternatively, as Steve Jones of the Sex Pistols said in 1978, 'It's got nothing to do with music, you silly cow!'

TABLE 4.3 Benny's Burgers Problem Map®

	Headline problem #1	Headline problem #2	Headline problem #3	Headline problem #4
Headline problem	I need to feed the family and I'm just too tired to cook today.	The weather is lousy and the kids are driving me nuts!	I'm pushed for time and the kids need feeding.	How do we mark a special occasion for the whole family?
Resulting problem 'A'	I become even more irritable and tired as I have to cook the dinner.	I am becoming increasingly short tempered as I have run out of things that we can do together.	I end up running late for an activity or meeting.	I don't want a bad atmosphere because someone isn't having a good time.

	Headline problem #1	Headline problem #2	Headline problem #3	Headline problem #4
Resulting problem 'B'	I start to feel a bit depressed as the chores never seem to end.	I am scared that someone is going to get hurt soon because the kids are getting increasingly wild as they become more frustrated.	I end up cooking a microwave dinner, which I really want to avoid.	I need to find somewhere affordable. We can't keep spending loads of money when going out. It becomes prohibitive.
Resulting problem 'C'	My mood is having a bad effect on the rest of the family.	I am sure we are going to have a family argument in a minute and there is going to be a bad atmosphere because everyone is just pent-up and stuck indoors.	I'm getting stressed out and this is leading to arguments in the house.	I don't want the occasion to pass by and do nothing.

KEY-POINT SUMMARY

- 'Ask not what your marketing can do for you but what your marketing can do for your customer.' Marketing is now an end in itself. It must create value in its own right.

- Benefits merely focus on transactions, dispensing reasons as to why a customer should buy a particular product or service. They will not help in creating value around what you do because they do not provide an insight into the universal issues that your customer experiences.

- When people search for information online, they normally have an issue in mind. For example, they may enter cinema listings into the Google search bar, but their concern is what they will be doing at the weekend.

- By thinking in terms of problems that your customers face, it is far more likely that your communication will resonate with them. In so doing, it will become much easier to engage.

- Problem Maps® provide a mechanism for understanding your product or service through the eyes of a potential customer. This insight then enables a business to create value around their core offering and subsequently enable them to engage customers and prospects alike.

- The key to engagement is always to put the customer first, by making sure that all communication is relevant and provides value.

CHAPTER 05

Products to experiences

Before the Second World War, the Western industrialized economies were product economies. More people were employed in the making of products than any other sector of the market. Differentiation, when purchasing, was mainly based on the quality and characteristics of the product. There was very little else to be taken into consideration when making a purchase. In a world of limited choice, customer expectation was relatively low.

After the Second World War the Western industrialized countries began to develop into service economies. By the end of the 1950s more people were working in the service sector than anywhere else.[1] As availability of products increased and subsequently prices reduced, they became increasingly commoditized. It was, therefore, the service delivery around these products that became more influential when making purchasing decisions. This new emphasis was borne out by companies that started to change the focus of their business. For example, IBM consciously repositioned itself from being a manufacturer of products to a service company delivering business solutions.[2] Customers were less concerned with the quality and features of a particular product as they became increasingly similar. It was other aspects of the purchase, such as free delivery, home installation or the availability of post-sales support etc, that became important when deciding on which item to buy.

Today, technology and the internet are changing where the perceived value in a purchase lies. Technology has enabled individuals to start businesses with very little capital investment. This is compounded by the new economic realities of the world in which we live. One of the major motivations in working for others was job security. However, today, even the biggest corporations cannot offer the same job security and guarantees of yesteryear. The result is that one of the major barriers preventing people from starting their own business, ie the perceived risk involved, has, to a large degree, been removed. There are, therefore, more people starting companies at home or working from small offices than in any previous age.

With an increase in suppliers and therefore more choice for customers, services have largely become commoditized. This has led to companies offering their customers progressive levels of convenience, speed, support etc, the result being that customers' expectations rise as profit margins fall. This has led to whole areas of service being outsourced. Outsourcing is a way for companies to provide services for their customers, for example 24-hour telephone support, while still making healthy profits, because it lowers the cost of delivery.

Offshoring is another trend attempting to achieve the same outcome. For example, many Western companies started to base their call centres in countries such as India. However, in many ways, this has resulted in the acceleration of the commoditization of service. As more companies outsource services to similar business-processing outsource companies across the globe, their focus is on delivering acceptable levels of service at an affordable cost, rather than creating anything special. Thus, over time, whole market sectors are delivering a similar service, from a similar provider, thousands of miles from where their customers live.

The internet has, perhaps, been the final stage of this commoditization of services. The speed and convenience that the internet provides make it a primary resource for the sourcing and purchasing of both products and services. However, the internet also creates commoditization as both products and services are distilled into similar, easily accessible promises which make the same claims regardless of the company.

With the emergence of comparison websites, products and services are condensed into comparable tables of analytics; in other words, delivery, date, availability, colour, price etc. The internet has also, in many cases, lowered the cost of delivery. The result of all of this is that customers put less value on good service; it becomes merely something that they expect.

For example, with the emergence of sites such as Amazon, service delivery has become incredibly efficient. Customers can choose to pay for 'next day delivery' or, alternatively, wait a few days at no cost. Whatever the option, customers can follow the progress of their package online. From the moment the product is ordered to its dispatch and its progress through the system until its final delivery, your package can be traced at all times. Once service delivery becomes this efficient there is nowhere else to go. As an increasing number of companies deem it necessary to offer this level of service, it becomes expected and commoditized. With the amount of choice customers have, they know there will always be a supplier, somewhere, who will deliver what they require. As companies try to compete online, the effect of all this is that often the only clear differential on the web is price.

The move from selling products to services did not affect the traditional transactional model of marketing. Instead of shouting about a product's benefits, companies merely emphasized the service delivery aspects of their offering, in order to entice people to buy. The messages, however, were still about the transaction: 'this is what you will receive when you buy'.

'Sticky marketing' does not work by shouting about the benefits of a transaction. Instead, the funnel is turned upside down and customers are attracted to your business. Once attracted to you, engagement can take place and, over time, many prospects will become customers. However, in order to attract prospects, value that relates to the products and services you provide is created. Communications are not merely about the transaction itself.

Whether you sell burgers and chips, accounting services, management consultancy, jewellery or anything else, people will be no more interested in your service than they are in the product unless they are in the market to buy. Ultimately, understanding how I will be looked after as a customer matters only at the point at which I want to find a provider.

The value is in the experience

In short, while products have been commodities for a long time, technology and the internet have commoditized services. This has led to a shift in what customers now hold in high regard. The value is no longer in the product or service that you deliver to a customer, but in the experience that they receive when engaging with your business.

For example, a restaurant in an amazing location and with a wonderful view will be able to charge more than an equivalent restaurant that lacks these other assets. Although the food and service may be the same, the experience will not be. The restaurant providing the view will be able to charge more for giving its customers a superior experience – and customers will be willing to pay for it.

Take passengers who fly business class. They still arrive at the same destination at the same time as those flying economy. Is it worth paying significantly more money simply to receive extra legroom? But of course, this is not what customers are paying for at all. Business-class passengers receive a faster check-in and a quiet lounge. Once on the plane, they enjoy a comfortable seat with more legroom and a better quality of food and drink. On landing, they disembark first and their luggage receives priority, thus minimizing their wait. Customers are paying for a whole experience which leaves them less tired and more relaxed than many of the passengers in the economy-class cabin.

Of course, one could argue that paying for better views in restaurants or for a superior flying experience has been happening for many years. This is true. The difference, however, is that today the experience is the primary aspect that matters. It is where the value exists. In a world before products and services were commoditized, the main concern of the majority of people was being able to 'join the party'. In other words, when Henry Ford offered customers a car only in black,[3] they didn't care. By reducing the cost of production, Henry Ford gave many

Americans an opportunity to own a car, something they could not have done previously. In this context, the aesthetics of colour were of little concern.

With the commoditization of products and services, this is no longer the case. In the Western industrialized world, apart from the most disadvantaged in our society, the majority of individuals can attend 'most parties'. For example, going abroad for a vacation is no longer the prerogative of the rich. In Europe, since 1992, low-cost air travel has been available to most people. The difference between flying with a no-frills airline or a more expensive alternative is not about the destination one can visit. For example, they both fly to Madrid. Neither is it about safety, because both airlines comply with the same safety regulations. The difference is whether one is given an allocated seat, the amount of legroom assigned, whether the chair reclines, the in-flight service of food and drink, the availability of facilities such as films and entertainment and the offerings of newspapers and magazines. In other words, the difference between the two is the experience.

Whether it is being able to buy modern technology such as computers and mobile phones, or being able to enjoy leisure activities such as meals out and visits to the cinema, price is no longer a barrier for most people. There is normally a solution available in all price brackets. Moreover, many similar products or services charge very similar prices. The difference between these today is more subtle.

For example, with mobile phones and computers it may be the aesthetics and usability of the particular device. In leisure activities, it may be the comfort of the seats, the view on offer or the quality of the ingredients. In other words, there is no value in enabling us to partake in these activities; most of us can. The value comes from the nuance within the offering; in other words, the experience provided.

Developing the experience

So, in order to avoid being commoditized and to be able to embrace the new engagement model of marketing, companies need to move away from products and services into delivering experiences. For example, take our two similar restaurants. Merely communicating the benefits of the food and service will not engage a customer. These aspects become interesting only when they are looking for somewhere to eat, having made an active decision to buy. Moreover, it is likely that both restaurants will make very similar claims as to the quality of their food and service, making it difficult to tell them apart. However, the magnificent grounds in which the first restaurant is located may make it a wonderful setting for a romantic meal. It may be this aspect that the restaurant decides to deliver to its patrons, ie 'give your partner the ultimate romantic experience'.

By focusing on this, the restaurant will then concentrate on achieving the right ambiance, using lighting, décor, music etc. However, to deliver a proper experience becomes all-encompassing. The romantic idea will necessarily influence everything from the food that is served (more meals for two to share) to the names of the dishes. Whether it is what the staff wear or their training in interacting with the clientele, everything must be taken into consideration. It is only by looking at all aspects of the restaurant's communications, with its customers, that it can ensure the idea is executed well.

Once the restaurant defines itself by delivering the ultimate romantic experience, it can then look to create value around this offering. The restaurant could position itself as a hub for romantic experiences in the area. It could provide tips, articles and fact sheets giving people ideas on how to mark important occasions for that special someone. These could be made available on its website. It may also be able to supply this information to other businesses that would find it valuable for their customers. For example, local beauty salons and spas may be willing to carry some information by providing articles or tips in their waiting rooms. By partnering with flower shops, beauty salons, chocolate suppliers, jewellery stores, luxury spas and agents for romantic holidays and weekend breaks, the restaurant could make it easy for customers to act on its suggestions.

Moreover, the restaurant could host themed evenings featuring ideas such as live music, chocolate indulgence or romance from other cultures. In this way, the restaurant would have content and offerings with which it could build an active engagement with a growing customer database. This experience, however, would not be merely about the food or service that the restaurant provides. In today's world of choice, they *have* to be good. On their own, though, they are not enough to ensure the restaurant's popularity. For the engagement model of marketing to work, an experience must be delivered. From this, wider value can be created which provides a reason for customers and prospects to want to interact with a business.

The importance of strategic partnerships

This example highlights another aspect of the engagement model of marketing. That is, you do not have to, and you probably cannot, do it alone. Partnering with other companies enables you to deliver value and maintain an engagement with prospects and customers alike. By taking this approach, engagement can be continued at very minimal cost. Meanwhile, your strategic partners have their own opportunities for business development, which otherwise would not have existed.

This is in stark contrast to the old model of marketing. Traditionally, a company would have products or services to sell. Having identified a target audience, it would then shout at these people. Those who became customers might then, in the future, receive special offers. However, all of this messaging tended to be transactional. It revolved around purchases being made.

This transactional model of marketing relied on capturing attention at the moment a prospect was ready to buy. Today, communications regarding products and services are less likely to be noticed at the appropriate time. This is because, as customers, we have been empowered. The ubiquity of available products and services, together with the access to information that we all enjoy, means that these marketing messages provide us with less value than ever before. Modern technology has increased the channels of communication available to us all. It has also meant that communication is no longer isolated to when we are behind our desks or in our homes. People make phone calls from their cars, send e-mails from the train, text while walking down the street and surf the internet while standing in queues. Consequently, the most precious resource a company can acquire today is customer attention. The companies that receive regular attention from prospects and customers will be the real winners in this technological age. Whereas traditional marketing valued the transactions that could be made as a result of a campaign (return on investment) today, successful companies should measure the ongoing engagement they have with their prospects and customers (return on engagement).

Therefore, partnerships are a vital ingredient in making your marketing 'sticky'. They allow a business to provide more value to its customers and prospects. This increases the likelihood of them remaining engaged. In turn, this becomes a self-fulfilling prophecy. The more engagement and attention any one company has from its customer base, the more value it can bring to potential partners who will, therefore, be more receptive to entering into an alliance. This provides a business with two opportunities: 1) to be able to keep adding value, through strategic partners, with little cost; 2) there is potential to earn passive income from any transactions a partner makes through your business. Of course, this would depend on the nature of any deal established.

Experiences are not limited to any one aspect of a company's offering. Whether it is engagement with a prospect before any purchase has been made, or whether it is interaction with a customer during or after a sale, experiences need to be delivered. For example, Amazon allows you to rate the books it sells on its website. This adds another dimension to a customer's reading experience. It provides them with a platform to deliver their own personal view and response to reading a book. Merely giving customers this platform demonstrates that Amazon believes that its clientele matter. This sharing of opinion also provides a better experience for potential purchasers of a book. Would-be customers, on the Amazon site, have the opportunity to learn from the wider community before making a purchase. This development of providing experiences, by supplying customers with a platform to become involved, is not confined just to the internet. For example, some of the most popular television shows of the past few years, such as Big Brother, Britain's Got talent, American Idol and X Factor, all have one aspect in common. The audiences are encouraged to have a say by voting for their favourite contestant. In other words, the outcome is decided by the people, rather than by TV producers. This involvement, however, is not restricted merely to voting on the programme. Both during the show and afterwards, viewers remain engaged, commenting on blogs, forums, in tweets and on social networks such as Facebook.[4]

Embracing the idea of providing experiences

The delivery of experiences is not confined to any particular type of business. Nor does it matter whether you are working in the business-to-business or business-to-consumer marketplace. All companies need to embrace the world of experiences if they want to flourish in this brave new world in which we find ourselves.

For example, our car dealer from the previous chapter wanted to engage with the local business community. It is for this reason that it volunteered the use of its showroom for a Chamber of Commerce gathering. The event, with guest speakers and networking amongst the different models of car, was an experience in itself. The challenge for the car dealer, however, is to make an everyday visit to the showroom an experience. The following example is one way in which this can be achieved.

Every day, our car dealer has fresh Danish pastries and coffee delivered. Not only does this make the showroom smell great, but it also creates a very welcoming environment. WiFi is also installed. Every person who enters is offered refreshments and the opportunity to sit with a coffee and catch up with any work. The showroom has a large car park which is under-utilized. Our car dealer decides to invite the local business community to use the facilities at their convenience and free of charge. This offer is open to anyone, not just customers. As word of mouth grows, local business people pop in, enjoy a coffee and Danish, and do a little work. This is, of course, a great way of starting an engagement with a prospect. Not every person who uses the showroom will buy a car from this dealer, nor is it expected of them. However, it is very likely that any business person who has used this showroom, when contemplating the purchase of a new car, will at the very least have this dealer in mind. Moreover, the goodwill and trust developed between this dealer and the business community will mean that more people will be predisposed to purchase from this showroom than would otherwise have been the case. Of course, it is not just the local business community who enjoy the showroom's facilities. When bringing their car in for a service, existing customers can also utilize the comfortable surroundings. This factor may be taken into consideration when making a purchasing decision.

On buying a car, customers are welcomed to one of four quarterly cocktail events, during the early evening hours, at an exclusive local hotel. They are invited to bring a guest, which introduces new potential customers to the showroom. As people meet and talk at these events, they will naturally exchange business cards; they remain in contact. To facilitate people staying in touch, regular networking events are held in this car showroom. These events are open to the wider business community in order to network and meet local business people. As a result, there is real value in the experience that this car showroom provides. Customer interaction is no longer only about the cars, or the service, that this dealership offers. Or, as in our prologue, 'It's got nothing to do with music, you silly cow.' Rather, it is the whole customer experience that people enjoy and value. It is much bigger than just the purchase of a car.

Participation

Delivering experiences makes engaging with customers before, during and after a transaction easier. The major difference between a service and an experience is simply: a service is something that is done to you or for you. An experience, on the other hand, is something that is done with you. In other words, the customer becomes integral to the solution offered.

Without the customer's participation, the offering would not be as good. In the UK, a football match has always been an experience because the fans' participation is integral to the event itself. First, there is the tribalism of fans walking towards the stadium, parading their team's colours. Once in the ground, there is the roar of the crowd when the teams appear, and the distain and euphoria exhibited on the different refereeing decisions. Whether it is the banter between the two sets of supporters or the cheers when a goal is scored, the event would not be nearly as exciting without the participation of the crowd.

Similarly, the difference between a good meal and a great meal at a restaurant is often not the food. At some establishments, aside from ordering the food, we may feel that we are almost superfluous to everything else that is happening around us. This makes the food merely a service for which we have paid. Alternatively, there are other times when we will feel engaged and very much part of the ambiance and atmosphere around us. This is when a meal can turn into an experience for which we will return on another occasion.

Delivering an experience requires customers to participate and become involved with your business offering. Whether it is reviewing a book, voting on a television show, stopping at our car showroom to eat coffee and Danish and make use of the WiFi, or attending an event, experiences require customers to actively participate. Today, this is reinforced by our increasing use of the internet to undertake our day-to-day activities. The internet, itself, is a medium which requires participation in a way that communication channels such as radio, cinema and television never did.

The internet encourages participation

The internet is the first many-to-many communication tool. It empowers all of us to 'get involved'. Unlike with previous communication channels, on the internet people do not want to absorb information passively. Rather, they want to comment, contribute and share. In other words, participate. Therefore, in order to engage with customers in any meaningful way, companies need to visualize the experience they provide, rather than thinking only in terms of the product or service they deliver.

There is an inordinate number of ways to develop experiences. Holding events around your product or service, like our car dealer, is one way of creating an experience. For some businesses, starting a club that provides events and special offers, and connects different members, could also be a way of delivering an experience. Clubs create a sense of belonging and community, which, if utilized properly, can be extremely powerful. User-generated content (UGC), ie allowing and encouraging customers to contribute content to your website by providing the wherewithal to comment on blogs and forums, or post their own articles, podcasts and video, is another way of engaging customers. Alternatively, giving customers an increasing influence over the products or services your company offers becomes part of the experience itself. This can be voting on an outcome, like in a reality TV show, or providing ideas that contribute to the next offering that your company provides.

Not only does participation move your business into the realm of experiences, but it also makes it more probable that you will be well received by customers. People are much more likely to embrace solutions to which they have contributed. Moreover, it is more conceivable that you will be talked about and, therefore, will achieve more positive word of mouth. Because experiences are internalized, they are emotional in a way that products and services are not. They are therefore much more likely to affect a customer. It is because they feel personal that they develop into a story and narrative more easily than do products and services.

Imagine going into our car showroom, buying a car and driving it away. You may tell a few people that you bought a new car, especially if you are pleased with your purchase, but it does not develop into much of a story. However, this changes once the showroom delivers an experience. Being offered fresh coffee and Danish, while sitting and catching up with a few e-mails and realizing that other people use the showroom as a business hotspot, becomes more of a talking point. Being invited to an event with food and drink at an exclusive hotel starts to provide you with a narrative that you are more likely to relate to others. Experiences, by their very definition, should be memorable. They have a greater impact on us than do products or services because they affect our feelings. Being more emotional, interesting and story based, we are more likely to talk abut experiences than we are to mention a product or service.

Today, the two main ways in which people source new products or services are online and by word of mouth, asking their network, friends, family, colleagues etc. It is hard to have much control over passive word of mouth, that is, people mentioning your business because they are pleased with the work undertaken. Providing experiences for your customers creates a reason for them to talk about you, therefore making awareness of your business by word of mouth much more likely.

Marketing's move from tactics to strategy

This highlights another important change between the old transactional funnel model of marketing and today's engagement model advocated by 'sticky marketing'. Because the traditional model of marketing was solely about the transaction, it was largely approached tactically. In other words, marketing departments would spend money on particular campaigns. An individual campaign might utilize TV, radio, billboards and mail shots. All of these channels might have delivered a consistent message for the campaign's duration. After the campaign was over, and having reflected on the results, new tactics would be employed, with some successes repeated. The same process would be undertaken at all companies, whatever their size. However, while big companies could afford to utilize channels such as television, smaller companies, especially in the business-to-business environment, would make more use of the letterbox and trade magazines.

Today, however, although occasional tactics can still be employed, marketing is no longer tactical but strategic. When people are buying experiences, the marketing is no longer something that you decide upon after the product or service has been developed. Rather, it has to be built into the design of your product or service. In a connected world where people have a plethora of channels in which to communicate, word of mouth is of the utmost importance. Therefore, a key question that needs to be answered in a modern marketing strategy is: How do you enable people to share whatever it is you do?

This is not something that can be bolted onto a product or service after its design. It has to be integral. It means allowing people to participate and get involved. For example, Amazon allows people to share their experience of books. YouTube also has word of mouth built into its offering. By allowing anyone to upload content for free, people accept the YouTube branding on the screen. This means that as people share their content, they are also spreading the word about YouTube.

In order to make your marketing 'sticky', it has to be truly aligned with, and part of, the business strategy. This was not always the case. Years ago, the leaders of a business would agree their strategy and the parameters of their product or service offering. Marketing would then be brought in to promote the offering using certain tactics. Today this is no longer effective. In order to be 'sticky' and engage prospects and customers, the promotion and selling of the product or service must become part of the experience.

For example, when our restaurant with the magnificent view decided to position itself as the ultimate romantic destination within its locality, this was as much a marketing decision as it was a product and service offering. Subsequently, partnering with beauty salons, spas, florists etc, as well as producing tip sheets and ideas for romancing a loved one, has as much to do with delivering an experience as it does with marketing. In other words, the two are seamlessly intertwined and are not two separate entities.

The changing dynamic between sales and marketing

This approach also renders another old rule redundant, that is, the splitting of the sales and marketing department. Traditionally, directors and senior management would set a strategy and decide the company's products and services. Marketing would then be brought in to communicate the virtues of the product or service to a particular target audience. Sales people would then be sent out into the field, to follow up the leads generated by the marketing activity. They would also capitalize on any market awareness generated by the campaign. This may appear to be a little simplistic, but in the business-to-business world, in essence, this is how it worked.

Today, marketing is integral to the business strategy. The experience ties up so many facets of the company's offering. Both the core products and services and strategic partnerships will affect the experience delivered. However, other decisions, such as how customers can share what you do, and how they can participate, will also contribute to the experience they receive. It is hard to distinguish between the different aspects that contribute to the experience, and the marketing is necessarily tied up in all of this.

'Sticky marketing', that is, cultivating a model of customer engagement, requires companies to attract prospects to them. Hence, the top of our upside-down funnel is narrow. The days of shouting at hundreds, thousands or even millions of people, in order to make them take notice of your offering, are disappearing. The logic of this is that traditional sales people are no longer required. These are the staff who would go out and, metaphorically, knock down doors looking for opportunities in the market. They were often known as 'hunters'. In many ways, the 'hunters' were an extension of, or were sometimes used instead of, traditional shouting.

The 'farmers', those sales people who were better at nurturing relationships over the long term, may still be required. This will depend on the nature of the business and whether it is cost-effective to employ what amounts to account managers in the field. Where this is applicable, these 'farmers' become more of an extension of the marketing department. In other words, there may be a point where initial customer engagement naturally leads to a face-to-face meeting being required. This necessitates marketing and sales to work much more closely together than has often been the case. In fact, when engaging customers, by delivering value over a long period of time, it will not always be clear where marketing stops and selling starts.

The lines between marketing and sales are now blurred in a way that they were not previously. In order to do a good job, both functions have to understand the other and work closely together. Today, so much customer engagement takes place online that you can often take a customer right through from initial interaction to a sale, and over time, upsell and cross-sell as well, just on your website. For example, a prospect may stumble upon the Amazon website while looking for a particular book on a given subject. In the first instance, it may be the book reviews that provide value and draw the customer in. Providing this value may lead this particular person to make an initial transaction. Over time, because of its sophisticated backend, Amazon may upsell other relevant books to this particular customer. As the company establishes credibility and trust with this client it may, in turn, cross-sell an electrical item such as a digital camera. A marketer involved with the internet interface of any business will need to have a deeper understanding of selling than they once did.

Meanwhile, a salesperson's role will need to change in order to repeat the customer engagement model in person. While marketing must ensure it is 'sticky' and engage customers via media channels, a sales executive must achieve this person to person. Sales people, too, must become 'sticky' and engage customers around the value and experience they can provide. In order to do this, they must be subject experts and, therefore, a useful resource to prospects and customers alike. Word-of-mouth recommendations, referrals and new customers will result from this approach.

Without understanding business strategy and marketing strategy, sales people will be unable to fulfil this role properly. So much of the customer engagement model requires the giving of value to customers around the transaction. Traditionally, sales people were focused only on the transaction. This requires a mind shift and change of emphasis in a salesperson's role. If it is relevant for your company to employ sales people, they are on the front line talking to prospects and customers every day. Their feedback and market intelligence can make a significant contribution in keeping your customer engagement model fresh and relevant. In other words, today sales and marketing should be working within the same department, taking on different roles, but utilizing the same strategy, and working closely together.

What has been, in many companies, an adversarial relationship has to change to become highly collaborative to the point that there should not even be two departments, but one. Today, sales has a large marketing function within their role, and marketing a large selling one.

The role of delivery mechanisms

The move from products and services to experiences requires a company to rethink the way it conceives the offerings it provides. It also makes it necessary for a business to reassess the role of both its sales and its marketing functions. It is also vital that a company considers the mechanisms by which it delivers the experience to its clients. When buying a product, whether one buys it at the store or orders it via a catalogue, the product itself remains unchanged. However, if businesses are no longer selling products or services, but experiences, the way in which a particular experience is delivered changes the nature of the experience itself.

For example, if you arrive home from work one night and do not fancy cooking, you may decide to get a takeaway. You will then make up your mind whether you want, say, Chinese, Indian, pizza or fish and chips, which may be the options available in your area. What is unlikely is that you decide to get a pizza and only then make up your mind whether you want a takeaway or to eat it in a restaurant. A more probable scenario is that you will decide whether you want to go out to eat, pick something up to bring home or have something delivered. In other words, in this example the delivery mechanism is more important than the product. Once you have decided how you wish to receive your food, only then will you decide on the particular meal. In a world of abundance of choice, we no longer buy products or services, but experiences. In this context, the delivery mechanism becomes a vital part of the experience. So:

- Some customers would like to buy in shops, others will want to buy online.
- Some will do research in shops and buy online and others will research online and buy in a shop.

- Some people will buy a whole album, some people will want only a single song.
- Some people will desire a physical CD with artwork, others will require a digital file.
- Some people may want to buy a book, others may want only one chapter.
- Some people may not wish to own the book but will pay a small fee to read it.
- Some people may not want to read the book at all but will buy the audio version, others may be happy having access only to edited excerpts.

In other words, by making your offering accessible in as many ways as possible, you can appeal to a wider market. Although the product being delivered may be the same, the experience will be different. Because of the low cost of distribution created by the web, it is often possible to distribute a product in a number of different ways.

For example, a management consultant may deliver their knowledge face to face with their clients. However, they could also offer a more general version of their expertise via phone seminars and webinars. It may also be possible to offer the principles that they espouse through a distance learning course sent via e-mail or accessed with a special code on a website. Other media channels such as podcasts and videos could also be exploited to impart some of their wisdom.

The general principle is this: while the knowledge stays the same, it can be packaged in a number of different ways. This enables people to access the information in a form, and at a price point, convenient to them. Some people may not wish to pay for face-to-face advice, but will be happy to part with less money and undertake a distance learning programme. Others may not be inclined to listen to podcasts but may be very willing to watch videos. A management consultant can take the same knowledge and, by packaging it in a variety of ways, can begin to deliver a very different experience to an array of customers. The web allows for the distribution of all these distinctive products at minimal cost. However, by being able to take the same knowledge and turn it into a number of separate experiences, our management consultant can maximize the revenue they are able to generate through their expertise.

The move to experiences is a direct result of the ubiquity of products and services. We are all faced with a plethora of similar choices, to which the internet has provided us easy access. It is in these circumstances that customers change their perception of value. With wide availability, consumers have stopped focusing on the products and services themselves. With regard to these, they have an expectation level which is already set extremely high. Rather, today, the real value is in the nuances that a company delivers. These subtleties, however, are not about product features and service deliverables, but in the experience a customer enjoys.

Once businesses focus on providing experiences, rather than products and services, opportunities to engage with prospects and customers transpire. This, in turn, allows a company to create value around its core deliverable and become attractive to its marketplace. Once a company realizes that its focus should be on providing experiences, it requires new questions to be considered and answers to be found. While these fresh challenges may make individuals feel somewhat uncomfortable, the opportunities that the move to experiences affords provides business with exciting prospects for the years ahead.

KEY-POINT SUMMARY

- Value is no longer in the product or service that you deliver for a customer, but in the experience that they receive when engaging with your business. The only way to avoid commoditization, and to be able to engage with your clientele, is by delivering experiences.

- Strategic partnering with companies will help enable a business to deliver value and maintain engagement with prospects and customers alike. Partnerships allow a company to create more value around what it does, which aids the process of becoming 'sticky'.

- Delivering experiences makes engaging with customers before, during and after transactions easier. An experience is something that is done *with* the customer. In other words, the customer becomes integral to the solution offered.

- User-generated content (UGC), that is, allowing and encouraging customers to contribute content to your website by providing the wherewithal to comment on blogs and forums or post their own articles and videos, is a great way of engaging customers.

- Giving customers an increasing influence over the products or services your company offers can become part of the experience itself. This can be voting on an outcome, like in a reality TV show, or providing ideas that contribute to the next offering your company provides.

- Today, marketing is integral to the business strategy. When people are buying experiences, the marketing is no longer something that you decide upon after the product or service has been developed. Rather, it has to be built into the very fabric of the offering.

- When buying a product, whether one buys it at the store or orders it via a catalogue, the product itself remains unchanged. However, if businesses are no longer selling products or services but experiences, the way in which a particular experience is delivered changes the nature of the experience itself.

CHAPTER 06

Unique selling point to customer engagement points

The idea of the unique selling point[1] or the unique selling proposition (USP) started to be used in advertising in the 1940s. It was finally written about and explained by Rosser Reeves, an advertising executive working for Ted Bates and Company, an advertising agency on New York's Madison Avenue. In his 1961 book *Reality in Advertising*, Reeves explains what the USP is and how it works.

In simple terms, a USP is a unique benefit that will attract customers. It is 'unique' because it is supposed to be an offer that no one else in the marketplace has. Therefore, it is a way of gaining a competitive advantage.

In the 'transactional funnel' approach to marketing, the USP was a great idea. If you are going to shout at people about your product or service, having something unique and therefore special gave you a greater chance of catching a prospect's attention. Moreover, your advertising, direct mail, leaflet drops etc were designed to capture people who were currently in the market to buy. Having a USP gave them a reason to buy from you.

In a world where there was relatively little choice, it was easier to come up with a benefit that was truly unique. With many services being restricted by geography, it was also possible to copy what a company was doing somewhere else, but still be unique within your own locality. However, the abundance of products and services, and access to knowledge and choice, which technology and the web have provided, has now rendered the USP completely and utterly irrelevant.

The USP, in reality, is just another benefit of your product or service, albeit a unique one. However, benefits are benefits only when a person is ready to buy. Therefore, for most people, at any one time, your USP will be completely irrelevant. The result is that it is almost impossible to engage prospects around your USP. Meanwhile, trying to compete on a USP, by definition, means making your offering transactional. It is also an easy way to get into a competitive race within your market, which can lead to commoditization, as competitors make greater promises to customers in order to attract business.

This highlights another problem with the USP. Today, there are hardly any truly unique offerings. With very few exceptions, there is almost nothing that you can conceive that a competitor cannot duplicate. The internet and the speed of communication allow ideas to be copied very quickly, resulting in your having no competitive advantage at all. In fact, often, all companies are left with are the additional costs of the new promises they made to prospects.

For example, in 2008 one or two companies came up with the concept of selling mobile phone packages by giving away free Netbooks as an enticement.[2a, 2b] However, the idea spread quickly across the globe to the point that it took very little time before there was no competitive advantage at all. Quite simply, what started out as a USP soon resulted in another customer expectation as they knew there would be someone offering a free Netbook when looking for a new mobile package. Not only did this not result in any significant increase in competitive advantage, but the aftermath was that companies incurred additional costs, however minor these may have been.

James Dyson patented his invention of the bagless vacuum cleaner. However, there are a variety of bagless vacuum cleaners manufactured by other companies available in the marketplace today. Microsoft owns Windows, but there are plenty of other office suites of software that one can obtain. Original ideas spread and are rewritten, changed and regurgitated by others. In other words, there are very few occasions when a company will have a USP for very long.

Moreover, it used to be possible to copy a USP, but deliver it in your own locality. Today, with the internet breaking down geographical boundaries, companies increasingly find themselves competing with businesses from further afield. The result is that even delivering something unique in your own area is becoming unlikely.

Why the USP will not sell experiences

The unique selling proposition requires a company to define its offering in a single idea. That is, a unique benefit that will attract customers. This is unhelpful in an experience economy. Experiences are more three-dimensional than products or services. Rather than being defined by one single idea, experiences often weave together a tapestry of ingredients which, as a collective whole, then deliver something special. However, each constituent part may *not* be unique in its own right.

So, in a previous chapter, Benny's Burgers developed a strong identity as a children's brand and became a hub for kids' activities in its local area. Similarly, our car showroom became a focal point for local business people. Experiences allow companies to create powerful market positions for themselves. Over time, this results in providing a business with competitive advantage. This is because, once a company has engaged a client base around a particular experience, a competitor has to be able to offer something significantly better in order to move that client base from the current supplier. This is not easy. The reason is that the more engaged a customer becomes, the more a business learns about the preferences of individuals and the customer base as a collective. This, in turn, allows a business to develop ever more personal experiences and relevant offerings for its customers. Therefore, constant customer engagement creates an ever-increasing barrier to market, as the minimum offering a competitor has to provide becomes harder to deliver from a standing start. The development of an experience allows for a company to become special and attractive to customers. This is not achieved, however, by trying to produce a defining USP.

For example, I am a user of Moonpig.com, the online greeting card company. When I send a card to family or friends, the site offers to remember the occasion and sends a reminder a few days before the event the following year. Over time, it has an extensive catalogue of dates and addresses, which means that no matter where I am in the world, I never forget a special event. Now, although a competitor site could offer a similar service, it would take a complete year of events to be able to offer me the level of service that Moonpig already delivers. Because of this, it is unlikely that I will leave unless I become particularly dissatisfied with Moonpig. However, as long as it continues to deliver, I am unlikely to look elsewhere. Meanwhile, because Moonpig allows me to personalize cards, altering the wording and adding pictures, it turns a very standard purchase into more of an experience.

As products and services become increasingly commoditized, the value in an offering is in the experience provided. Companies can no longer define themselves by a single USP. For example, is there anything a solicitor can offer its clients in terms of product or service that cannot be copied by another firm? Probably not. In the old transactional model of marketing the USP was fundamental to the offer being made to prospects. It was *the* reason to do business with you rather than anyone else. Today, 'sticky marketing' requires the focus to move from transactions to customer engagement. Businesses have to start thinking in terms of experiences provided, rather than products or services delivered. Companies previously attempted to gain attention by developing an irresistible USP. Today, companies must become attractive by using entirely different criteria. We must move from thinking in terms of unique selling points (USPs) to creating a vision based around customer engagement points (CEPs). Customer engagement points are a way of transforming what you do into a multidimensional, tangible entity, which engages customers in a number of ways and on a number of levels.

The journey to customer engagement points

However, in order to arrive at the customer engagement points, we are required first to answer a different question. A business will be able to introduce compelling CEPs only by undertaking a process that will enable it to reach the right answers. The first part of this process is the completion of a Problem Map®, as introduced in Chapter 4.

It is vital to understand that every purchase solves a problem at the point at which it is made. It may be that, later on, a customer regrets buying a particular item or service. However, at the actual time of acquisition, a problem will have been solved. This could be a practical purchase such as buying milk so that one can have a cup of tea or buying petrol to run the car. Alternatively, it could be an emotional purchase; for example, buying an expensive watch to solve the problem of establishing or maintaining status, or a luxury car which enables the owner to demonstrate their success. Shopping has also become a displacement activity in modern times. In other words, the mere act of going to the shops to buy something solves the problem of not having anything to do or anywhere particular to go.

The Problem Map® is a mechanism for understanding both the emotional and practical challenges that your potential customers will face. Once a Problem Map® has been completed, the starting point for making your business attractive is to ask the following question: Why are we best placed to solve the problem? The answer to this question requires you to look at your Problem Map® and think about the following four areas:

1 What is the actual problem that you solve? Although your Problem Map® will cover a wide variety of issues, there will be key themes and problems that continually recur. These will indicate what the fundamental and overriding problems are. It is these issues on which you must focus your attention at this juncture.

2 For *whom* are you best placed to solve these problems? This question will help you distil who your likely customers will be. You must consider the people who are most likely to face these issues. You should also contemplate for whom the solving of

these challenges will be most compelling. By understanding this, you will be able to identify the particular clientele for whom you can add the most value. In order to be able to achieve the right answers, you must also consider when these problems are likely to occur, and where these people are likely to be at that time.

3 What are the current dynamics of the market? It is important to identify the sectors and localities in which you wish to operate and the offerings that already exist within those places. By understanding the choices already available, you will be able to carve a distinguished path for your own business.

4 Is there anything special about you? Whether you are a one-person business or a vast organization, companies have to assess if they already possess experience or expertise which makes them particularly attractive to certain types of customers, within specific market sectors or locations.

Having clarity in these four areas is fundamental to any marketing strategy. If you do not know why you are best placed to solve the problems for a specific set of customers, *they* will never know. It will be impossible to define your customer engagement points properly because you will not have the clarity around whom you should engage and why.

CASE STUDY   Example case study

We can see more clearly how this works by taking an example of an accountancy firm. Having completed its Problem Map® it decides upon the fundamental issues it believes it solves for its clientele. These are:

- Compliance: There are a number of obligations a company must fulfil. Failure to do so leaves them vulnerable to severe penalties or even prosecution. Many companies do not have the in-house expertise to deal with these issues.

- Financial security: Valuable insights can be gained from understanding the financials of a business. Without these, companies can put themselves at risk by missing fundamentals, such as cash-flow, profit margins etc.

- Missed opportunities: Companies must constantly evolve in order to maintain competitive advantage. A detailed reading of a business's accounts can assist in identifying new opportunities on the one hand, and areas that are becoming less productive on the other.

Having understood the fundamental problems that this accountancy firm solves, the second question that must be answered is: Who is most likely to have these problems? It is also important to consider when and where these challenges will occur. Our accountancy firm will use the experience of its current customers to enable it to develop its answers:

- Who? Chief executive officers, managing directors and finance directors are the main people who face these issues.

- Where? Financial issues can play on people's minds wherever they are. However, they are particularly focused upon them in their place of work.

- When? These issues will come to the fore at specific times. For example, they will be given particular consideration at year end. Alternatively, other events such as a company not developing as hoped, or a business with ambitious plans experiencing problems with cash flow as a result of rapid growth.

The next area our accountancy firm considers is the dynamics of the marketplace and its role within it. If this accountancy practice is a two-partner firm, it may decide that its market is local. People often like to have their accountants close by. There is also no point in trying to work with customers who are 200 miles away from its office when there are plenty of clients for a two-partner firm on its doorstep. So, it decides that its marketplace is a 30-mile radius from its office. Within this area it understands which other accountants exist, from the corporate firms down to some of the smaller firms like itself. Who are they? What do they offer? What are the profiles of businesses within this 30-mile radius? What do they look like in terms of turnover or number of employees? Are there any particularly strong market sectors within this area?

On preparing this research, the firm realizes that there are a large number of small accountancy practices and they all present themselves as general practice, all-purpose firms. It also realizes that the majority of businesses in the area are small owner-managed companies without employees. There are also a significant number of small entrepreneurial businesses with a small number of employees.

Finally it looks at itself; what is special about the two partners? One of the partners previously ran their own business and so has a very good understanding of the dynamics of being a small business owner. The other partner has a lot of experience of working with start-ups and helping them grow. The two accountants recognize that their experience is with small entrepreneurial businesses. There are plenty of these within the 30-mile radius in which they are happy to work. They understand, therefore, that their customers are going to be small business owners. Within their 30-mile radius there is no accountancy firm that has positioned itself as *the* accountant for entrepreneurs.

Therefore, the answer to the question 'Why are we best placed to solve the problem?' is that in their locality they are the only specialists working with small entrepreneurial businesses. This is an area in which they have vast experience. The point of the positioning is this: they are not best placed to solve the problem for everyone. In a world with an abundance of suppliers, no one can be. However, for their target audience of small business entrepreneurs, they are the best placed firm to solve the problem.

This can sometimes be as much about perception as it is about reality. In other words, the core skills required to assist one market may be exactly the same to help another. However, it is vital that you define the market in which you want to operate. In a world of abundance, trying to be all things to all people actually means being nothing to anyone. Faced with so much choice, people will gravitate to a supplier whom they feel is exactly right for their requirements. In a world of so much choice, there is likely to be one. You must, therefore, decide upon your niche.

An engagement strategy means becoming attractive

An engagement strategy is about encouraging prospects to come to you. In order for this to happen you have to be attractive. There are two aspects to being attractive. First, you have to be noticed. It does not matter how attractive you are, if no one knows you exist. Second, you have to be desirable. That is, once you are noticed, people must be drawn into wanting to know more about you. In a world of choice, being a small fish in a big pond will not get you noticed. This is the equivalent of trying to be all things to all people where there are so many options available. On the other hand, if you are a big fish in a small pond, you will always be noticed. This is the equivalent of working within a defined market. The more relevant you appear to be to a particular marketplace, the more likely it is that they will see you as desirable.

Companies often become concerned when defining their market in narrow terms. The feeling is often that they are dismissing potential opportunities out of hand. This is not the case. It may seem counter-intuitive, but the narrower your market focus, the more attractive you become to a particular audience. Moreover, determining a narrow focus allows you to choose a market where you may already have some inbuilt competitive advantage. For example, by choosing to define its market as small business entrepreneurs, our accountancy firm's experience became much more relevant and important. Herein lies an essential lesson for all companies. In a world of abundance of choice, it is necessary to be a big fish in a small pond. Far from being restrictive, this can be liberating. After all, you get to pick the pond. Of course, why wouldn't you carve up a pond in a way that provides your business with maximum competitive advantage? When finding a niche, the only question a business must ask is: Is the market big enough to sustain our business? As long as the answer is yes, there is little to worry about. In fact, it may even be possible to define the market still further.

Being a big fish in a small pond will mean more word of mouth, more recognition and more customers. Once you dominate the market, if you desire, you can diversify by getting representation in offices in other regions, or moving into different vertical sectors. For example, you may start off defining your audience as doctors and slowly, over time, diversify into dentists. You may choose to do this with your existing company name or by creating a different brand.

The principle, however, is this: in an engagement strategy, aim at the narrowest target market to which you can give the best experience and which will sustain your business to the level you require. In our accountancy firm example, working with small entrepreneurial businesses, within a 30-mile radius of its office, provides a large enough marketplace. The other importance of narrowing your market is that it becomes a self-fulfilling prophecy. In our accountants' case, they have identified that their experience is in the field of small businesses and these are the customers with whom they will engage. The more they engage and the more customers they acquire, the more they learn and the more contacts they build in this area. This produces a virtuous circle whereby, as a result of working in this narrow field, they become increasingly valuable to their target market. As they continue to build their experience, knowledge and contacts, they become true experts in their area of specialization and increasingly capable of delivering added value to their customers.

This is also true for their geographical focus. While building knowledge of other businesses, they are able to introduce their customers to other sources of expertise in their locality, eg specialists who can help with the sourcing of funding. Thus their claim of being the best firm to solve the challenges of small entrepreneurial businesses in their area continually strengthens over time.

The importance of a 'narrative'

Once you have answered the question 'Why are we best placed to solve the problem?', there is another consideration before examining your customer engagement points. Part of understanding the experience you are delivering to customers is to explain the narrative behind what you do, how you started, or what you are trying to achieve.

For example, you may have a certain methodology that you use when working with a customer, which you may be able to explain in story form. Alternatively, you may be able to recount how you started in a back room somewhere and how you grew. This may be an interesting journey that a customer will enjoy and that builds your credibility. Conversely you may have really ambitious goals for what you are trying to achieve, whether it is feeding the starving or stopping the homeless problem. Building a story around these ambitions can help bring them to life and enable people to understand where you are coming from.

A narrative can become part of the experience for a prospect or customer. A compelling story can be engaging in itself. It allows people to understand you. In turn, this makes it easier for them to feel that they know you and can trust you. Stories often give prospects and customers something to talk about, making it more likely that your message will spread. Is it any wonder that the most successful book of all time, the Bible,[3] contains some of the best stories and narratives ever told?

Moreover, a narrative helps people internalize what you do. It has the ability to affect them on a deeper level than simply stating facts about your product or service. It enables them to feel part of your business, rather than simply being a bystander. In this way your offering becomes more personal. If companies need to deliver experiences, having a narrative sitting behind them will also make it much easier to deliver consistently, time and again.

Having understood the problems that you solve for a customer, you then define your market in order to ensure that, within your niche, you are well placed to be the solution provider. By being strategic in determining the markets in which you operate, you become a big fish in a small pond. This is the first stage of ensuring that you are attractive; that is, being noticed. The second part of attractiveness is becoming desirable. Desirability is achieved by imparting value. It is this that will encourage prospects to engage with your business. 'Sticky marketing' requires ongoing engagement with prospects and customers alike. In a world of abundance, we are all overwhelmed and distracted by the choices we face. Consistent engagement means having the attention of our prospects and customers. This makes it very likely that when they are ready to make a purchase we will, at the very least, be considered and on many occasions we will win the business. This return on engagement model requires a system for developing engagement strategies just as the USP provided a mechanism for developing effective ways of shouting at prospects in a previous age. Customer engagement points (CEPs) provide businesses with this formula.

Introducing customer engagement points

Customer engagement points comprise four areas:

- partnerships;
- content;
- market positioning;
- emotional selling proposition.

Partnerships

While partnerships, alliances, associations etc are as old as business itself, the purpose of these is now changing. In the old traditional transactional marketing model they had limited use. They existed when both parties felt they could achieve more sales when working together than on their own. Partnerships were also about maximizing profit. So, for example, the alliance[4] between McDonald's and Coca-Cola gave McDonald's a competitive advantage by serving the world's leading cola brand in its restaurants. It gave Coca-Cola access to a huge audience on which it may otherwise have missed out. Both parties found the arrangement highly profitable. This agreement, however, was not about engaging the customer, rather it was transactional. The fact that Coca-Cola is available in McDonald's is only of interest to me when I'm thinking about buying a fast food meal. While it may influence my purchase at the time, it will not engage me at any other moment.

Today the abundance of choice and information available, together with the fragmentation of media and communications, has rendered attention a scarce resource. This means that companies already enjoying prospect and customer attention need to find new ways of providing value in order to keep them engaged. This can often be achieved by partnering with aligned businesses. The focus of these partnerships, however, is in creating value in order to maintain customer engagement and keep their attention. For companies that do not enjoy the attention of their potential marketplace, they have the opportunity to leverage a business that has succeeded in this area. Therefore, a win–win situation ensues. While one company can use partnerships to add value and keep its customers engaged, another can use these partnerships to develop some initial interaction with future customers. While, indirectly, both companies will hope that this partnership increases sales over the long term, that will be an indirect result of the alliance. The initial criterion for determining the partnership will be to create customer value which, in turn, will encourage both prospects and customers to engage.

Understanding with whom to partner takes you right back to your Problem Map® and the issues that you solve. For example, in Chapter 4, Benny's Burgers realized that it was not in the business of burgers and chips but in the business of activity displacement for children. Therefore, it looked for other companies that were in the activity displacement for children business. This led to a partnership with the local zoo, leisure parks, cinema etc. Engaging customers around burgers and chips was almost impossible. People would be interested in its offering only at very specific times. However, having activities to amuse your children is a perennial and universal problem. Benny's Burgers could not fix the problem on its own but by partnering with other businesses it widened the solution it could deliver by offering vouchers for these other activities. It also broadened the experiences which it could assist in bringing to its clientele. Vouchers, in themselves, are not an experience. However, by enabling the different experiences at the zoo, cinema, bowling etc to happen, Benny's Burgers became a small part of the occasion and benefited from some of the goodwill generated. Partnerships allowed it to deliver value and become a hub for parents looking for things to do with their children. Thus partnerships are an important element of an engagement strategy.

Similarly, our accountants working with small entrepreneurial businesses could look at partnering with a solicitor, an HR consultancy, a marketing company or other service providers who also have small businesses among their clientele. With these partners, our accountancy firm could offer money-off services, fact sheets and top tips and hold seminars, all relating to assisting the small business owner. Thus engagement can take place by creating value through partnerships. This example with our accountants brings us to our second customer engagement point.

Content

Understanding the problems that you solve for a client can lead you to appreciate the sort of content that can be delivered, that will create value around your core product or service. For example, Benny's Burgers solved the problem of activity displacement for children. It partnered with other companies that solved the same issue and created offers for each of the activities. This was then turned into content, a flyer containing all the vouchers that could be downloaded from its website. Then, after the summer, Benny's Burgers created more content of value by distributing activity booklets for kids, via e-mail, on weekends when the weather report was not favourable. Imparting value like this helped to keep both the parents and the children engaged. It was never, however, directly about burgers and chips, or, as Steve Jones so rightly said, 'It's got nothing to do with music, you silly cow!'

Our accountants could use partnerships in order to create great content for their clients, together with their HR, marketing and legal partners. If you are a service provider with a vast amount of expertise, you can create your own material. Alternatively, you can partner with other firms in order to create something of real value for your clients. Suppliers may also be an important resource that you can utilize.

For many businesses, the most important contributors of all can be the customers themselves. So, for example, on Amazon, the content of real value is the reviews written by customers. These reviews offer useful insights when making a buying decision. However, this content would not be nearly as respected if it was produced by Amazon itself. The credibility and value come from the fact that contributions are made by regular readers. Moreover, by giving customers a platform on which to participate, a service turns into an experience as consumers are able to become involved.

Content can be made accessible on your own website or delivered by request directly to prospects and customers via e-mail, RSS feeds etc. However, accessing content on your website relies on visitors coming to you. There is no doubt that your website can be a powerful engagement tool. However, many opportunities will be missed if a business depends solely on this channel of distribution. You should not simply expect prospects and customers to visit your site.

Rather, a far more powerful strategy is to take your content to the places your prospects and customers already visit. This can be achieved by utilizing public platforms used by your customers, for example iTunes, YouTube, Facebook, LinkedIn, Twitter etc. It can also be accomplished by partnering with other businesses and associations. For example, a tip sheet full of great ideas produced specifically for small businesses by a solicitor may be uploaded onto their firm's website. However, because the content delivers real value and is not simply a promotional tool, associations like the local Chamber of Commerce and Institute of Directors may also carry the piece in their newsletter, magazine or on their own website. The top tips may also be disseminated individually over the course of a few weeks on Twitter. By taking the content to the places to which small businesses already refer, this content has a lot more chance of being seen and engaging new prospects. Links from the information could direct readers to other sources, such as the firm's website or blog, for those who would like to learn more.

Whether it is creating videos for YouTube, writing serious articles for other people's websites and portals, or encouraging customers to contribute material to your own website, content is an extremely important strand in building customer engagement points. The right content, together with the appropriate strategic partnerships, starts to contribute towards the third part of your customer engagement strategy.

Market positioning

'Sticky marketing' is all about attracting customers to you. With the abundance of choice and access to information that we all now have, there is little point shouting at prospects. People will do things when they are ready and on their terms. Creating an effective market position for yourself, and your business, is vital in becoming attractive.

Benny's Burgers partnered with other children's brands offering free discount vouchers. It designed and gave away children's activity booklets. It also created an excellent dining experience within its restaurant. In so doing it became one of the de facto children's brands within its area. It became a hub, a trusted adviser if you like, and the first port of call for parents when it comes to children's activities in the locality.

One of the myths in this world of abundance is that customers now demand, and want, choice. Consumers actually do not want choice at all. People often feel overwhelmed by the number of options they face when making a purchasing decision. What customers actually desire is the result that so many choices provide. That is, exactly what they want, where, when and how they want it. Therefore, people are becoming increasingly sophisticated about how they search for new products and services, in order to find what they are looking for as quickly as possible.

With so many choices available, people find ways of making sense of it all. They often achieve this by using filters, ie ways to screen out all the noise and find what is relevant to them. This, in effect, is what Google does. When you initiate a search, it screens everything else out and delivers the most pertinent results for you. Similarly, posting questions, and asking friends on social or business networking sites, achieves the same results. The recommendations that come back are delivered by trusted contacts and, therefore, are credible. By relying on these recommendations, you reduce the market from an overwhelming amount of choice to a few manageable options.

Within their own niche markets, many businesses can deliver this to their patrons through effective market positioning. For example, in its area, Benny's Burgers is becoming *the* filter for children's activities. Similarly, our accountants could do the same thing for small businesses within their locality. So, they could partner with the right business networks and advisers. By also providing good content and being involved in organizing some interesting local events, over time, they could become a hub for small business activity. In order to become a hub, the resources you provide must be highly relevant to a specific group. This reinforces the requirement to be a big fish in a small pond.

Market positioning is more robust than the USP. A USP can normally be copied with relative ease. Once that happens, it does not matter to the customer whose original idea it was. If two companies offer free delivery, do you care which did it first? However, market positioning is different. Benny's Burgers is not the only children's burger bar in its area. It has some very well-known competitors. However, it is Benny's Burgers that has the right strategic partnerships, regularly delivers valuable content to an engaged customer base and provides information about other children's activities on its website.

No business must be complacent. Nor should it take enjoying the attention of many of its prospects and customers for granted. However, if another burger bar in the locality did try to copy Benny's Burgers, while not impossible, it would face an extremely difficult task. Established strategic partnerships, good quality content – like their activity booklets – and an established reputation for delivering accurate and relevant information cannot be cultivated overnight. It is a slow organic process. Over time, the cost of implementing this strategy is minimal. However, to try to compete from a standing start is a huge challenge. Moreover, while copying free delivery or a giveaway or matching a price is relatively simple, trying to copy an experience is that much harder. Not only this, but experiences are internalized. This means that an emotional attachment is created. Therefore, delivering an excellent experience to your customers develops a deeper sense of loyalty than a mere product or service ever can. The importance of emotion in an experience economy brings us to our fourth customer engagement point.

The 'emotional selling proposition'

'Sticky marketing' requires businesses to engage people by creating value around what they do. This is achieved by understanding the problems that they solve. By providing content, working with partners and developing a market position, companies move away from merely delivering a product or service to providing customers with an experience.

An experience is emotional. It is internalized. It is three-dimensional. Delivering an experience can only be done effectively by understanding emotionally what you supply. Identifying the emotion that your company conveys will assist you in being able to produce an experience that is consistent. Do you:

- sell candles or romance?
- sell burgers or escapism?
- provide accountancy or reassurance?

The language on your website, the way your staff dress, your corporate colours etc should all reflect the emotion you deliver. The technological age has made word of mouth more important than it has ever been. People only recommend companies they trust. Therefore, in order for people to trust you, they must feel that they know you. By delivering an emotionally consistent message, you will become familiar more quickly and, therefore, are more likely to be recommended more readily and more often. Achieving consistency has become increasingly difficult when there are so many channels of communication available to us. Many companies and individuals find themselves in the position of maintaining a website, writing a blog, creating Facebook profiles and fan pages and having a LinkedIn profile, while Tweeting pertinent bytes of information etc. Not only this, but within businesses there may be a number of contributors to these channels. How do you maintain consistency across so many platforms? Your emotional selling proposition provides a useful internal benchmark and guide in order to help make this happen.

In order to arrive at your emotional selling proposition you need to ask yourself two questions:

1 What do the problems that we solve mean emotionally for people? Does our small business accountancy firm provide peace of mind, reassurance or security?

2 How do we want people to feel when they use us? Our small business accountancy firm may want people to feel calm or comforted. It is, of course, quite possible for two accountancy firms to have two different emotional selling propositions. Our small business accountancy firm, whose target market is entrepreneurs, will have a very different offering from another accountancy firm that specializes in preparing audits for public limited companies (PLCs).

Whatever your emotional selling proposition is, it should be one word. For example, hope, reassurance, empowerment, romance etc which will act as an internal benchmark for everything you deliver to your customer. It is not something that you share directly with clients; rather, it should come across in every communication and interaction with them. Your emotional selling proposition must be consistent with everything you are trying to achieve as a company, especially with your market positioning.

For example, Virgin is one of the most successful private companies in the world.[5] Although it was conceived over 40 years ago, it is still perceived by many as a fresh and exciting company. Much of this is due to its market positioning. Although it is a large and successful company, it is inevitably the underdog in almost all markets in which it competes. Virgin Records was not as big as the likes of EMI. In aviation, Virgin was up against national airlines such as British Airways. In mobile phones, Virgin competed against established brands such as

O_2 and Vodafone. Virgin, despite its own success, normally appears to position itself as the minnow, attempting to take market share away from much larger corporates. It is because of this that its entry into a market often seems quite exciting. It usually approaches the market with a promise to change the status quo. Therefore, emotionally, it delivers a feeling of anti-establishment.

This goes hand in hand with the persona of Virgin's famous founder, Richard Branson. We buy into the anti-establishment message because he is an unconventional business leader. While attending business meetings wearing casual clothes may not seem very radical today, it made quite a statement in the early 1970s. Meanwhile, his high-profile activities outside of the office, such as attempting the fastest crossing of the Atlantic in a powerboat and his adventures in a hot air balloon, mean that we accept the fact that he is not your typical executive of a large company.

By carefully fashioning a good market position, together with a clear understanding of the emotional selling proposition that your company delivers, you will enable your business to create a strong identity. By providing quality content and leveraging partnerships, the mechanisms will be in place to develop a robust customer engagement strategy. Continually providing value to both prospects and customers alike will keep them engaged. It may then be possible to become one of their trusted filters in your particular area of expertise. With consistent interaction, transactions will happen, over time. The key to success, however, is leveraging CEPs in order to create and maintain successful customer engagement.

- All companies must identify the problems that they solve and the customers to whom they could add the most value with their solutions. This, combined with an understanding of the dynamics of their marketplace, and the unique expertise their own business possesses, will start to lead a company towards an effective marketing strategy.

- The narrower a company's market focus, the more attractive it becomes to a particular client base. Determining a narrow focus allows it to choose a market where it may already have some inbuilt competitive advantage. The aim is to be a big fish in a small pond. The key is for a business to pick the right pond.

- Part of understanding the experience you are delivering to customers is to develop a narrative behind what you do, how you started or what you are trying to achieve. A compelling story can be engaging in itself. It can help people feel like they are part of the business.

- Customer engagement points comprise four areas – partnerships, content, market positioning and the emotional selling proposition.

- Partnerships can help create value in order to maintain customer engagement and, therefore, keep their attention. They can also assist a business in developing some initial interaction with future customers.

- Content can be made accessible on a company's own website and be sent to customers via e-mail, RSS feeds etc. A business should not simply expect prospects and customers to visit it. Rather, it is essential that content is also delivered to sites and platforms that a company's prospects and customers already visit.

KEY-POINT SUMMARY CONTINUED...

● Creating an effective market position is vital in order for a business to become attractive. The aim is for a company to become a hub, a trusted adviser, in its own specialist area. In other words, become one of the filters people use, in order to make sense of the overwhelming amount of information to which they are exposed.

● An experience is emotional. It is internalized. It is three-dimensional. Delivering an experience will be performed more effectively by understanding emotionally what a business supplies. Identifying its emotional selling proposition will enable a company to produce an effective experience that is consistent.

PART 04

COMMUNICATING

THE MESSAGE

CHAPTER 07

Messages to conversations

Before the internet, the major forms of communication – print, radio, cinema and television – left the public as passive receivers of information. The few people who had the means of distribution could convey their ideas to the many, and the rest of the populace had to be satisfied with sharing their thoughts with friends, family and colleagues.

Magazines and newspapers had letter pages and radio shows hosted phone-ins, but most people had very few ways of distributing their ideas to the masses. This being the case, it was something that the 'silent majority' accepted ('silent majority' being a well-known colloquialism that reflected this situation). In marketing terms, these circumstances gave companies quite a lot of control in their interactions with prospects and customers alike. Companies would create imagery and messages and then pay for distribution in order to put these in front of their audience. Consumers had very few outlets by which they could respond to this messaging and therefore were unable to voice an opinion.

Moreover, because customers had very little access to information regarding new products or services, commercial messages were often worthy of their attention. The development of technology and the internet has completely transformed this situation. We have come full circle, whereby control has shifted from companies to individuals. The general populace has now been empowered in a way never previously known. We are no longer passive receivers of messages, but active players in the creation of that information.

A good example is the news. Everyone used to glean their knowledge from the same few newspapers, television and radio stations. Now, we obtain information from a plethora of channels, including websites, blogs, forums and social networks. For example, during the protests following the Iranian elections in 2009, it was, at times, faster to get information about what was happening on the streets of Tehran by following a stream on Twitter than from any traditional news network. Similarly, insightful videos of protests were being posted on YouTube. This content was not being generated by news networks but by ordinary people who were participating in the protests themselves. Because of the volume of material that is being produced in this way, it is fairly easy to corroborate stories and therefore make sense of what is going on. Thus today, fast, accurate and reliable information is being provided by the masses. Others can, in turn, react to this in real time.

The news is obviously one example, but this phenomenon is happening in all aspects of our lives. Millions of people are now making music, videos or writing articles and books, all of which can be accessed by the multitudes. For example, it was through YouTube that Susan Boyle experienced global fame overnight when her appearance in the 2009 UK TV series 'Britain's Got Talent' was posted on that website and subsequently received tens of millions of hits.[1] British television made Susan Boyle a star in the United Kingdom. However, it was YouTube that made her an overnight global sensation. There has, in effect, been a democratization of the production and distribution of ideas. This phenomenon has directly impacted on the effectiveness of the traditional marketing approach that companies take.

Today, all consumers have a voice, and many exercise it on a regular basis. Having been empowered, customers now expect to be involved. The result is that people do not want to be 'marketed to' as they once were. They do not want to be passive. Companies used to be in control but this is no longer the case. Customers are no longer willing to sit back and simply wait to be shouted at by businesses. In fact, many of these messages are being screened out by viewers. Up until 2002, 78 per cent of consumers said that advertising was a good way to learn about new products. By 2006 that figure had already dropped to 53 per cent, according to *Business Week*,[2] and it is in steady decline.

Companies used to sell their products and services by devoting large budgets to shouting at people in order to direct them to their particular offering. In the world of technology and the web, customers will look for this information themselves. Predominantly, they will refer to two places. One is their own networks, that is, friends, family, colleagues and other online connections. The second is searching on the internet. Whether information is obtained face to face, on social networking platforms or by conducting searches, the knowledge imparted will be dominated by the opinions of individuals. Face to face, this will literally be via word of mouth. Online, this material will be disseminated through comments and postings, in forums and on networks, on blogs and in reviews written by consumers etc. A company's own messaging will be only a small part of the plethora of information available and may not be accessed at all.

Power to the people

In a world where we all have a voice, a growing number of us are not just passively listening, but partaking; that is, posting ideas, views and comments. This information is then available for everyone else to see. In effect, we are all now marketers, having the ability to communicate our likes and dislikes on a massive scale. Moreover, we are more likely to be influenced by the views of other consumers rather than companies themselves. We identify with other customers because we believe they are like us. Unlike companies, we also assume that they do not have any vested interest in the comments they make.

The internet has made information extremely transparent. Because we have so much access to information, we are all more savvy and more cynical. The age of bombarding consumers with attractive images and messages which they will passively accept is gone. The reality is that more marketing messages are created by the public than by marketing departments. Ultimately, people have more influence on brands than the companies themselves.

It is the contributions from ordinary people in the form of blogs, postings in forums, reviews, comments on Facebook or other social media platforms, Tweets etc where the real marketing is happening. These conversations are where the communication of ideas is taking place. It is here that people interact, influence purchasing decisions and become influenced by others.

This changes the whole nature of marketing. Customers are no longer pawns to be marketed to, for the sole purpose of generating transactions. A company's success is no longer down to how attractive a product or service can be made to look by a creative advertising campaign. The public at large now play an enormous part in the marketing of any offering. Previously companies controlled messaging, now the best they can do is help facilitate it.

There used to be an adage that 'the customer is king'. I would suggest that customers are even more important than that. Today, the customer is your partner. This is because, for a product or service to be successful, you now have to market *with* your customer, not at them.

Becoming 'part of the conversation'

Conversations are happening online, with you or without you, and power has shifted from companies to the public. The web will not help businesses identify customers who are ready to buy. The best that can be achieved is a cold list of data. All the research in the world is unlikely to reveal a company's or individual's buying intentions, or make them susceptible to any subsequent advances. What it will do is assist buyers in discovering suppliers who are ready to sell. In other words, you cannot find customers using the web, they have to find you, but with so much choice available they will probably not have to look too hard. This means that you have to make sure your business goes to where activities are already taking place. That involves participating in the conversation. However, for a company to move from the old system of shouting at people with messages, to the new paradigm of being part of the conversation, they will have to alter the way they undertake their marketing activities.

In the old model of marketing, messages were conveyed to the public by shouting at them through a variety of available channels. Companies may have conducted market research to try to ensure that their shouting would be relevant and well received, but that is often as far as any interaction went. Today, the emphasis is on conversations. These conversations often happen in real time and, like regular conversations, are at least two-way. As in any conversation, there will be subtleties and nuances that must be recognized. This, together with the speed at which messages can travel, means that companies need to be attentive. Businesses, therefore, before participating in these conversations, must be listening. Failure to listen intently can leave companies making inappropriate communications and damaging their reputations. Conversely, listening properly will give companies the opportunity to add real value to prospects and customers, and engage with them in a meaningful way. This engagement may well lead to transactions further down the line.

There are many online tools available that businesses can utilize in order to listen to the conversation. Understanding what is going on in the market will provide an array of opportunities. It may lead to developing new offerings, or delivering specific information, help or advice. All this creates value for prospects and customers. In turn, an engaged market will be more likely to purchase from these companies, at the appropriate time, and be more loyal to a business that always dispenses value in a relevant and timely way.

Starbucks was obviously monitoring the conversation when my friend Mark Shaw took his daughter for a drink in one of their branches. On Tweeting this fact, Mark was delighted to receive a message from Starbucks itself. It was genuinely interested in Mark and his view of the experience it provided. Having exchanged several messages with Starbucks, Mark is now a self-confessed advocate for the brand. Not bad, considering that he was a loyal patron of one of Starbucks' main competitors.[3]

There is a plethora of tools available which one can use to monitor the conversations taking place. A comprehensive recounting of all of these goes beyond the scope of this book. The following information is meant only to provide readers with an idea of the types of mechanism to which I am alluding. Google Alerts can be set up to monitor comments on particular subjects, brand names or topic areas. Similarly, one can search threads on Twitter using Twitter Search. Whether you look for your company name, subject of expertise or product area, you are likely to gain valuable insight into people's opinions, issues and concerns in the market. Monitoring relevant blogs, wikis and forums, as well as interest groups on Facebook and LinkedIn, will provide businesses with valuable knowledge. Blog search engines such as Technorati can also be useful tools in understanding what people are saying about your area of interest. As well as a variety of free tools, there are various text-mining technologies which can be used to monitor the web and are available for purchase.

These new tools give companies unprecedented insight into their marketplace. One must remember that consumers also have more knowledge than ever before. Therefore, with fresh opportunity come new risks. Companies that misrepresent their position or tell half-truths about their business are in danger of being exposed very quickly. Businesses that fail to listen to their patrons and provide them with real value will soon find they are ignored. Conversely, the businesses that do provide value, and therefore engage consumers, will benefit from a great reputation, word-of-mouth recommendations and, over time, an increase in transactions.

Companies can no longer simply broadcast messages at prospects and customers as they once did. Today, rather than control communications, they can help facilitate them. Facilitation means entering into a partnership with prospects and customers. Businesses can legitimately lead conversations if they have new ideas or research that they want to share. They can make suggestions and ask questions, and in this way help set the agenda. Businesses must remember, however, that individuals can do the same. They therefore must be prepared for conversations to go in directions that they did not anticipate. If companies operate ethically, are truthful and authentic and have a good sense of who they are and what they stand for, they have nothing to fear. In fact, the opposite is true. Unexpected conversations can often create options for businesses which they did not even realize existed.

The customer is no longer king, but your partner. Having a partner means allowing them to have a stake in your business. Although this may sound risky for many, companies today simply have no choice. However, with big risks also come big rewards. Once a prospect or customer feels that they have an influence on the company, they will then have an interest in its future. Thus, they are more likely to be loyal to that business. Many customers are willing to spend a lot of time and put in a lot of effort, not for financial reward, but because they want to. For many clients, participation is the prize. People no longer want to be passive, they like to have a say. Far from running away from this situation, it should be embraced. By facilitating this involvement companies can, over time, create a very loyal and vocal group of customers.

User-generated content and co-creation

Where appropriate, businesses should encourage user-generated content (UGC). That is, allow and encourage customers themselves to provide useful content that, in turn, helps to create value in your business offering. For example, one of the ways that SKY News adds value to its website is through 'SKY News Discussions', which facilitates people in voicing their own opinions on current events. Users can start their own discussions and respond to other people's points of view. This turns the SKY News website into an experience, as people are encouraged to get involved. These comments become a rich resource of the public view on any current event. Of course, SKY News has its own editorial pieces, but its site is much richer for ensuring that the wider public can also contribute. Giving people an active voice is empowering and encourages them to keep using the website. It also means that they are likely to talk about it in the context of their own post, and therefore promote the website to others.

There are entire websites whose value lies in the content contributed by the public. Both YouTube and Facebook are merely platforms that enable user-generated content to flourish. The value is in the information contributed by the members.

Another similar idea to that of user-generated content is 'co-creation'. That is, allowing customers to suggest new ideas as well as influencing the products and service that companies introduce themselves. If people are involved in creating and shaping your products and services, they are more likely to tell others. Moreover, by allowing customers to collaborate with your business, you enable them to customize what you do. Therefore, you are more likely to offer exactly what your customers require. Not only does this cut out inefficiency and wastage, but it also increases customer loyalty – customers may reject your solutions, but they are less likely to reject their own.

A good example of a company that has really utilized co-creation is Lego. Its 'design by me' website allows you to design your own Lego which is then shipped to you with all the bricks you require for your own creation. Furthermore, the most popular designs have been turned into real Lego products. Therefore, customers have the opportunity to produce proper Lego merchandise which will be sold to a wider audience.

Co-creation encompasses many elements, from allowing prospects and customers to design products and services from scratch, to enabling them to change aspects of the offer, such as delivery, colour, specification etc. One of the advantages that user-generated content and co-creation bring is that they encourage people to talk about your business. Those who are actively involved in the creation of a company's offering are more likely to spread the word and become advocates. This is significant. For, if you recognize the importance of the conversation, then a part of any company's marketing strategy is to build word of mouth into its offering. In other words, give people something to talk about.

For example, if you take the time to upload a video to YouTube it is because you want it to be seen. Therefore, most people who upload content to YouTube will send links to family, friends and colleagues. Similarly, no one wants to be on Facebook with no friends. Therefore, on joining, people will invite others to connect with them on the platform.

By creating iconic white headphones, Apple made sure that the marketing was built into the product. Anyone walking down the street with white headphones in their ears is presumed to be listening to one of their iconic iPods.

Building conversation into any offering is vital in order for it to succeed. Encouraging people to comment by giving them something to talk about or share is fundamental to any marketing strategy. Whether it is user-generated content, co-creation, multi-user games, competitions etc, every marketer should now be asking themselves: Where is the conversation for this product or service? Why would my marketplace want to talk about it? If the answer is that they wouldn't, something needs to change.

Identifying the 'influencers'

If conversations are now so important in marketing, understanding who is most likely to have the conversation, and whose opinion will carry most weight, is an important part of any marketing strategy. In any given marketplace there will be key individuals, who have more influence over potential buyers than others. These people are known as 'influencers'.

Influencers are normally those who are better connected in a given marketplace and whose opinion is taken seriously. They can be potential customers themselves or, alternatively, be a trusted third party. For example, accountants could be regarded as influencers in the purchase of financial software.

Whether these influencers are extremely active in a particular market, eg a well-known and followed blogger, or whether they are well connected or are considered trendsetters by their peers, it is worthwhile companies identifying who these people are, and how they can possibly work with them.

There may be communities of influencers who, despite not purchasing your goods, may be worth engaging. So, some IT consultants may be very influential in the enterprise software that a company chooses, even though they will not be buying that software for themselves. If this is identified, a software provider might look to engage the IT consultant community. Of course, it could only do this by providing those consultants some perceived value. This may be achieved with white papers, webinars or other events. In so doing, the software provider would be able to demonstrate its expertise and gain trust and credibility. This makes it more likely that it will be recommended by the IT consultants at a relevant time.

In identifying influencers, companies may have the opportunity to market straight to their customers. For example, a customer relationship management (CRM) software provider may identify marketing consultants as being key influencers in the purchase of customer relationship management software. It may strike up a partnership with these consultants and produce material, free trials and downloads that actually sit on the consultants' website. Thus, it is marketing straight to the clients of these consultants. The consultants themselves may receive commission on every purchase as well as feeling that this information provides added value for their own clientele.

Loss leaders can also be used in order to turn influencers into advocates. These could be in the form of providing them with exclusivity, hosting special events, or even giving your product or service away for free. In turn, if they like it, they may well become an advocate and tell others. People who are well networked in an industry or on social networks, an influential blogger or spokesperson in a particular community, will be the type of people for which this scenario may be given consideration.

For example, when Nintendo launched the Wii, this is exactly what it did.[4] Its Ambassador Program identified key market categories. Nintendo subsequently hosted events for each ambassador and their closest friends and relatives. This allowed those ordinary people to play with the Wii for the first time and then to share their experiences.

Years ago, influential journalists could make or break a new product or service with a positive or negative review. The difference today is that we can all choose to be critics in areas for which we are passionate. In the world of old media, most of us did not have the wherewithal to respond to a journalist's article. Today, we can all write reviews and respond to others'. Consequently, reviews often become catalysts for conversations to occur. Engaging with influencers can help a business become part of more conversations in more places.

A point to consider is that influencers are not necessarily individuals within your target market. They can also be people sitting outside of that group. So, consultants, industry bodies, procurement groups, bloggers, spokespeople etc can all have a huge influence on your customers' buying decisions without being part of your potential customer base. It is important that these people are considered in any marketing strategy as they may very well be part of the conversation whether you choose to engage with them or not.

The importance of social platforms

One particular type of platform where conversations will take place, and influencers will be found, is on social networks. When trying to engage with your market, you cannot expect those people to come to you. Initial engagement will often have to happen in the places they frequent. Consequently, businesses do need to utilize social networking sites, because whether it is Facebook, LinkedIn, Twitter or one of the many others, inevitably their customers will be on them. The offering you provide may determine the platforms that your company chooses.

Communities have always existed amongst people with common interests. These were once limited by geography and required belonging to a particular organization, eg a church, a school, a youth club, the Scouts etc, the biggest of these institutions of course being the nation state itself. Now, however, communities can be formed online, across borders and time zones.

Communities previously formed in geographical locations required a critical mass of participants in a relatively small area in order to make the group worthwhile. So, if you had a niche interest, you might have been able to conjure up only three or four people in your area who would want to participate in your group, thereby not making the proposition particularly attractive. Today, without these geographical boundaries, communities can develop more easily around niche interests. Without geographical limitations, even the narrowest interest groups can obtain enough of a critical mass to make it worthwhile.

Within the large social networks such as Facebook and LinkedIn, there are many communities, clubs and forums started by people with interests in narrow fields. There are, therefore, opportunities for companies to engage with all walks of life and also build communities of their own on these platforms. Developing communities, within these platforms, is another channel open to business which can be used to engage. It becomes another way of creating a hub and facilitating the spread of knowledge and ideas in order to impart value.

Companies that choose to develop communities must understand that, ultimately, they are not about the business at all and how many sales they might make. Rather, they are about the community and the wider value created by everyone within the group. Communities are comprised of people interacting and having conversations. Although a company may facilitate these forums and groups, it should not view it as control. It does not own them, and if it thinks it does, and it abuses its position, it will watch the community disintegrate. The dialogue must be allowed to develop of its own accord without a business trying to police it. Dialogue is necessarily two-way. It is, therefore, as important for a company to listen to what is being said, as it is for it to contribute.

Abusing social media and using it to shout at people in the old way, without allowing or caring about the response, is an abuse of what these communities are about. Companies that do this are in danger of ruining their reputation. Social media are not a forum for transactions. They are more akin to having a conversation in a bar. Transactions result as customer awareness grows, together with the credibility and trust that, over time, you earn.

Hard selling is not appropriate in a bar, neither is it appropriate in social media. It is not called 'social' for nothing. A good conversation in a bar is more likely to develop if you show an interest in other people. Conversely, if you show blatant disregard for other patrons, they will be insulted and are likely to bad-mouth you to others. Exactly the same will happen on these online platforms.

For example, a company with which I worked uses social platforms to engage with curators of museums. Rather than talk about the storage equipment that it actually supplies, its focus is on providing a forum for curators themselves to share knowledge through video, podcasts, case studies, articles etc. Related associations such as those concerned with antique furniture, coin collections and paintings are encouraged to share their knowledge and expertise. The idea is to create a hub with which curators will regularly engage. This, of course, does not guarantee that the company will win their business when they require new storage equipment. It will, however, mean that curators are aware of its services and will likely give its solutions at least some consideration. Moreover, the goodwill and trust this company acquires will mean that many curators will be predisposed to using this provider if possible.

Businesses must understand that marketing today is about providing an experience. That often involves creating value at the periphery of your core offering. As part of this engagement, knowledge can be shared on social media platforms. For example, on business networks such as LinkedIn, where people often ask professional questions, information of value can be imparted. In so doing, however, companies should not try to sell, the same way as they wouldn't in a bar. If you are having a drink in a bar and someone asks you a business question, you will most likely give an answer of value and then say, 'if you want to know more, give me a call and we can have a meeting', and then offer them your business card. You will most probably then carry on drinking and have a good evening with the person, which, incidentally, will make it much more likely that they will get in touch.

The same is true of online social networks. Engage with people and focus on giving value, so that people enjoy their interactions with you. Instead of giving your business card, you can often provide an answer of value and then refer to further sources of information; these may include your website or blog, for example. The irony is that by not focusing on transactions, over time, you will probably get more of them.

Marketing today is not about delivering clever messages but about having good conversations. As well as contributing, it is equally important to listen and learn from them. Good conversations allow companies to educate their marketplace, provide value, demonstrate their credibility and expertise, and therefore, over time, elicit trust. The most important sales people and marketers a company has today are often not those whom it employs but rather, those who become advocates. Conversations enable ongoing engagement, which, over time, leads to sales.

Marketing, however, has moved from being a message to being a conversation.

- Today everyone is a marketer, having the ability to communicate their likes and dislikes on a massive scale. It is in the contribution from ordinary people in the form of blogs, postings in forums, reviews and comments on social media platforms that the real marketing is happening. The reality is that more marketing messages are created by the public than by marketing departments.

- Companies have to move from the old system of shouting messages at people to the new paradigm of being part of the conversation.

- Before participating in conversations, businesses must be listening. Failure to listen intently can leave companies making inappropriate communication and damaging their reputation. Conversely, listening properly will give companies the opportunity to add real value to prospects and customers and engage them in a meaningful way.

- Where appropriate, businesses should support user-generated content. That is, allow and encourage customers to provide useful content that in turn helps to create value in your own business offering.

- Co-creation means allowing customers to collaborate with your business. It encompasses many elements, from allowing prospects and customers to design products and services from scratch, to enabling them to change aspects of the offer, such as delivery, colour, specification etc.

- In any given marketplace there will be key individuals who have more influence over potential buyers than others. These people are known as 'influencers'. Companies should identify who these people are and ways in which they may be able to work with them.

KEY-POINT SUMMARY CONTINUED...

- Businesses do need to utilize social platforms because whether it is Facebook, LinkedIn, Twitter or one of the many others, inevitably these are places that their customers regularly frequent.

- Marketing has moved from being a message to being a conversation. Consequently, an important part of a marketing strategy is to give people something to talk about. Building conversation into any offering will inordinately increase the chance of success.

CHAPTER 08

Image to reputation

The Industrial Revolution made it possible to mass produce products; mass media made it possible to shout about them. It was these phenomena that led to the traditional funnel approach to marketing that became the accepted practice and wisdom.

Products were mass produced and distributed. Companies would then shout about them in order to grab people's attention. Constant shouting would ensure that these goods were very much in the public consciousness. As items were required, people would often trust products that were most familiar. Because of this, it was the products that companies paid to shout about that were usually the most successful.

Traditional mass media meant that a company conveyed its message to an audience, who were reduced to being mere passive receivers of the information. Customers did not often interact with any person from these corporations at all. Companies in this world of one-to-many communications needed to try to re-create the feelings that a person had when they bought from someone they knew and trusted.

Take a product like Coca-Cola. The majority of people would never actually have interacted with anyone from the company. People bought the product from distributors: local stores, supermarkets, 24/7 outlets, bars, hotels etc. In these circumstances, companies needed to create a sense of loyalty without having the luxury of a personal relationship with their customers. This resulted in modern branding. That is, giving a label, name or product a personality by which the public could create an emotional attachment and, thereby, create loyalty.

Of course, it was not real. Products, labels and logos cannot have personalities. They are merely illusions. With this approach, in traditional marketing, image became vital and was the way that consumers were influenced, especially for many companies that had no direct contact with their customers. Businesses spent millions of dollars employing agencies and marketers to devise communications that would create a brand image into which consumers would buy.

Of course, consumers knew that products and labels do not really have personalities. However, there are some simple explanations as to how this form of communication became accepted. First, there was not the transparency of information that there is today. Numerous companies would convey false images about their products. For example, many food manufacturers would use nostalgic imagery of traditional local suppliers delivering a wholesome and natural product. The reality, of course, is that many of these items were produced in large factories and full of chemicals and additives. Although, at a basic level, consumers knew that these adverts were not real, without the wherewithal to easily question the imagery, or the means with which to voice an opinion, most people just accepted the message at face value.

Second, there was nothing else. All companies, to a greater or lesser extent, could only get their message across by shouting. In other words, everyone was playing by the same game and by the same rules. As customers, we did not have easy access to information. However far-fetched or tenuous some of the advertising was, it was insightful in informing us about what was available in the market. Therefore, somewhere within these messages, value existed. This being the case, we were more predisposed to accept these communications.

Moreover, a lot of advertising involved attempting to give personalities to labels or inanimate objects. This was an effort to create loyalty in lieu of any personal contact between the company and their customers. Obviously, as consumers, we understood that these objects did not really have personalities. The whole premise was slightly absurd. For example, an excellent and highly successful UK TV commercial from 1974 was for Cadbury's Smash mashed potato.[1] In it, a group of robots recount their visit to planet Earth and speak of their observations regarding human behaviour and their consumption and preparation of potatoes. In a world where adverts included such bizarre scenes as talking robots, any allusions to claims that were not true did not seem quite so incongruous.

Finally, the context of delivery was also very important. Communicating via billboards, magazines, newspapers, radio, television, direct mail, cold calls etc was all very intrusive. This was because, in essence, you were interrupting people while they were trying to do something else. Because the medium was so crass, people's expectations of the message were not high. In essence, companies did not have to pretend that they were doing anything other than shouting at people to sell their merchandise. With hindsight, one can see that this form of communication was invasive and somewhat obnoxious. However, there were no real alternatives and so everybody was doing it. This, coupled with the fact that there was some value for the consumer, meant that people just accepted it. However, because this shouting was slightly disagreeable, people did not think of holding companies to a higher set of standards. In other words, if you were paying to interrupt and then shout at me, I did not expect anything more than propaganda from you.

How we all became marketers

However, with the onset of technology and the internet all of this has changed. Customers now have an abundance of choice, an abundance of access to information and the ability to have a say. Image and branding were invented to give products a personality, to replace the people-to-people interaction that originally took place before products were mass produced. It was an attempt to create some sort of loyalty. However, today people-to-people communication is once again happening. Marketing is now two-way. Companies have the ability to engage directly with consumers on a highly personal level. Similarly, customers have a variety of accessible communication channels through which to contact a business.

Consider this. There are more people than company representatives. Therefore, there is likely to be more material – that is, blogs, comments and reviews – written by customers or potential customers than from a company itself. Moreover, consumers are more likely to take notice of what other customers say than any communications from a business. As consumers, we believe that something written by another customer is more likely to reflect the reality of the experience. We assume, in most cases, that other customers have the same interests as our own, have no axe to grind, no agenda and nothing to sell. Therefore, although marketing is people to people, the company is often not even part of the conversation taking place, which is a completely new phenomenon.

For example, tripadvisor.com is a website used by travellers to source information on hotels, flights, restaurants and other ideas for excursions. Perhaps, however, the most valuable aspect of the site is the comments written by those who have already experienced the various offerings. With so many choices available, it is unlikely that travellers will book a hotel that has a couple of scathing reviews.

In a world of abundance of choice, we all need to filter the information available, in order to decide on the most appropriate solutions for us. Word of mouth from friends or other people's reviews and comments help distil down the wide amount of material to a manageable level. However, this is no longer about an image that a company creates. Image does not get you good feedback or positive comments and reviews. You achieve that through a good reputation. In other words, modern marketing has moved from being about the image that companies create to the reputation that companies have.

Brand value has been spoken about by marketers for years and is vitally important. Brands can be worth millions of dollars and have real equity. The importance of the brand has not changed, but the ingredients have. Brands have often been a company's greatest asset, based on the image that has been created and reinforced. Today, a brand may still be the greatest asset a business has, but now it is based on a company's reputation.

Marketing is a conversation

Now that communications are many to many, marketing no longer consists merely of a company delivering messages to a passive receiver of information. Rather, it is now an active participant, 'the company', engaging with another active participant, 'the customer'. Moreover, communications can be delivered by one active participant, 'the customer', who, through blogging, writing comments or posting reviews, can convey a message to another active participant, another 'customer'. In other words, customer-to-customer as well as company-to-customer communications.

This means that marketing is undertaken less by traditional messaging and more in the context of conversations and discussions. In reality, this means that much of a company's marketing will be done by others, whether it likes it or not. Today, we know about companies, not because of the image they project, but through comments, conversations and discussions. In this world image matters less. Reputation, however, is vital.

Of course, it does not mean that image can be completely neglected. Companies still need to make an effort in this regard. However, the point is this: with image, what was most important was what a company said about itself. In a connected internet-enabled world, where conversations matter, the most important factor is what others say. This is not image, but reputation.

Image is directed by a company itself, but a company cannot control the conversation. It can participate, it can add value and comment, it can even facilitate discussions, but it cannot control. For example, Google yourself and see the search results. Did you know everything that is there? Do you know everybody who has written something? You can try to manage your reputation and it is vital to do this, but you must remember that people will participate on their terms and not yours.

One of the ways of greatly influencing your own reputation is by dominating much of the content about yourself. Owning your own profiles on industry networks, eg Chamber of Commerce, Institute of Directors and any trade associations, is vitally important. The same is true for big platforms such as Facebook, Twitter, LinkedIn etc.

Providing great content will not only help you engage with people, but will positively enhance the reputation that you have. Winston Churchill once said: 'History will be kind to me, for I intend to write it.'[2] In a internet-enabled world this is very apt, and today it could be changed to read: 'People will find good content about me, for I intend to provide it.' While providing valuable content and plenty of it will certainly help in developing your reputation, just as Churchill could not write every history book and control everything that is written about him, neither can you.

Building credibility and demonstrating expertise and knowledge, by supplying good content, will enhance your reputation. It is more important today than any image you may create. As more people produce their own blogs, videos and podcasts, we are willing to put up with a less polished production, as long as the content is good. A lot of this home-recorded material conveys authenticity and is, therefore, often very well received. Thus, where a well-produced slick image might have been enough before the internet, now, even more important than image is content. In fact, producing something too slick can be counter-productive, as it may lose the human element and then may no longer seem genuine.

The move to authenticity

This move towards genuine, authentic and real is another result of the internet-enabled world in which we now live, and the move from image to reputation. What customers are buying today are experiences. However, in an experience, the customer becomes part of the offering. For example, think about the crowd at our football match in Chapter 5. Without the crowd, there is no excitement. In other words, the crowd is an important part of the occasion. Delivering an experience requires customers to make more of an emotional investment than is true of products or services. They, inadvertently, become 'stakeholders' in your business. The result is that companies have to reflect the values of their prospects and customers. They have to match their customers' perception of themselves and who they are.

Think how passionate football supporters become about off-the-field business decisions made by the board. This is because of the emotional investment that supporters make when following their team. The same is true of any experience. For example, Gary Glitter was a very popular musician in the 1970s, with millions of fans. Many of these fans, however, will feel unable to play his music today because he is now a convicted sex offender. Because experiences require an emotional investment by the customer, in a way that products or services do not, a company's values and beliefs will be examined and considered far more closely by customers than they were previously.

Potentially, this can provide a business with the opportunity of having a more loyal and committed client base, if the business's values align with those of its customers. However, it also brings risks. Customers will not want to invest emotionally in companies and offerings they feel are fake or based on trickery. Old marketing often relied on companies developing an image which was rarely based on reality. Buying was emotional in that it was aspirational, but it rarely required people to give something of themselves. The few experiences that were on offer, such as football matches or pop concerts, did require this. This, perhaps, goes some way to explaining why we have always been so critical of our pop stars, holding them under a microscope. This is because we feel like 'stakeholders' in their lives, having invested emotionally in them. However, most products or services did not require much of an emotional investment and, therefore, companies were able to convey a false image purely invented in the marketing department or advertising agency.

However, because customers communicate directly with a business, the traditional marketing approach now seems a lot more like lying than it once did. Companies can no longer be something that they are not. When businesses went out into the market and shouted about themselves, customers did not expect more than a phony advertising message. However, today, a lot of customers' interaction with your business will be at their behest. They will have taken the time to ask their network for a recommendation or will have found you by searching on the internet. When customers go to this much trouble, investing time and effort in the process, they expect something genuine.

Moreover, when marketing was purely transactional and existed to grab people's attention, everyday images were not best placed to achieve that. Rather, exaggerated imagery would need to be used. Grandiose claims would frequently be made, often completely removed from reality, in order to seize the attention of the consumer. By its very nature, this is not a genuine approach, and in today's market a company that works this way is unlikely to achieve the successes of yesteryear. For example, Vaibhav Bedi brought a case against Unilever in India[3] for the 'depression and psychological damage' caused by the lack of any 'Lynx effect'. Whether this brings a wry smile to your face because, as a sophisticated consumer, you assumed the 'Lynx effect' never existed, or whether you feel he is right to sue over a product that, in his opinion, has failed to deliver on its promise, it demonstrates the problem with traditional advertising. That is, in order to stand out from the crowd, companies magnify the results of using their products or services.

When marketing is about engagement, rather than transactions, it requires a company to provide value rather than just a phony image. There needs to be substance and content. To produce value requires a genuine approach, something more authentic. This is because marketing is now part of the experience, not separate from it. Previously, marketing was one step removed from the product or service people bought. It was simply a vehicle for driving the customer to the offering and nothing more. However, if you are selling experiences, this changes. Every single interaction and message from your company is part of the experience.

Communications in trusted networks and social media

The whole point of 'sticky marketing' is to engage with prospects and customers over a long period of time. This requires a business to constantly provide a valued experience. The way interactions now occur affects the tone of communications and renders the traditional marketing approach irrelevant. Today, an increasing number of conversations are taking place within trusted networks and social media. These are communities where every individual is firmly in control of their profile, the messages they write and the ones to which they respond. Because they are social, companies have to act in a social way. Think of other social places, like a bar or a pub. A company representative would not just walk into a bar and shout about what they do. Needless to say, they cannot do this in the context of social media, which is personal and discussion based. These places require a higher standard of behaviour from business, an honesty and integrity perhaps not required on a billboard or TV commercial. Moreover, niche communities that exist within platforms such as Facebook or on their own sites are created around values. Therefore, it is incumbent upon companies to reflect the values of the community with which they would like to become involved. Similarly, companies will not be able to truly engage customers and build their own communities without reflecting the values of those people they are looking to attract.

This becomes increasingly important within the context of word of mouth. We trust other customers, bloggers and reviewers more than companies themselves. There is a plethora of ways for people to access the recommendations of others and for all of us to show the wider community our likes and dislikes. Blogs, forums and review sites are just a few, as are websites which allow people to tag their favourite articles, videos and other content. Among these are sites such as Digg, Sphinn, Reddit and StumbleUpon. The more advocates a company has and the more passionate people are about its business, the more likely positive word of mouth will occur. People will not go out of their way for you unless they feel they know you and like you.

This is the antithesis of old marketing. It requires the stripping away of the outdated obsession with creating desirable, yet unobtainable, imagery which develops expectations that cannot possibly be met. Instead, 'sticky marketing' requires a transparency, honesty and authenticity which, quite frankly, most companies are just not used to offering. With marketing being peer to peer, rather than company to prospect, and consumers having more of an influence over people's perceptions of a business than ever before, this is now the only approach that will prove effective. Having advocates, as well as being part of, and building, communities, will contribute to generating positive word of mouth. It is about establishing a good reputation. This requires substance; it is not about image.

For many companies this also means not being obsessed with trying to be perfect. Businesses that are too slick can put customers off participating. This is because, if something seems complete and perfect, there is little point in anyone else contributing. However, not pretending to have all the answers will encourage engagement and participation. Empowering people, and genuinely asking for their input, makes it more likely that they will want to become involved. Allowing users to generate content and customize offerings is a great way of becoming an experience, as well as being seen as authentic. Crowd participation, by definition, is genuine.

The importance of values

This also forces businesses to think about their values as never before. In an image-based world, where customers bought products and services, values were not nearly as important as they are today. Now, customers buy experiences and are, therefore, more emotionally involved in a company's offering. In this environment, reputation is key. For businesses, this means that they have to stand for more than merely making money for their shareholders. There has to be a higher purpose. By a higher purpose we are not necessarily referring to a philanthropic aim, such as feeding the hungry or housing the homeless, although, for some companies, this may be applicable. Rather, higher purpose refers to a vision, to a company's reason for delivering its solutions.

So, Benny's Burgers' higher purpose could be to assist in making the most stimulating and vibrant activities accessible to every child in its locality. Aspects of this had already been achieved through partnerships with other businesses, such as the local cinema or zoo, which resulted in being able to provide discounts on these activities. At other times, Benny's Burgers fulfilled this mission itself; for example, by producing activity booklets for children during the winter months. This purpose, while not necessarily stated publicly, would guide the way the company operated. In turn, consumers would have a sense of what Benny's Burgers is about. This is something bigger than simply making money.

Similarly, our small business accountancy firm's aim may be to try to ensure the success of every entrepreneurial start-up within its area. Some of the partnerships it establishes and seminars it hosts may help towards this goal. Its purpose would be something that could excite the small business community in its locality, as well as guide its future actions.

People cannot rally around making someone else money. In order for a business to have meaningful values, it must understand its purpose, that is, what lies at its essence. Today, all companies need to think about their vision at a much deeper level than many have previously. In order to identify what this is, businesses must put the customer at the centre of everything they do. Built into any solution should be the wherewithal to enable people to contribute. Providing consumers with the mechanism to generate feedback and ideas will assist a company in staying vibrant and delivering something authentic and exciting. In so doing, customers will be more likely to want to engage and talk about the business. This is in stark contrast to how companies traditionally operated; that is, looking internally for answers and, on producing them, shouting at consumers, hoping they would buy.

Developing a narrative

One aspect that can help businesses understand who they are and engage customers is their narrative. That is, the company story. Good speakers engage their audience by telling stories. This is because they can often capture the imagination, providing a context and perspective which can be easily remembered and understood. Meanwhile, developing a narrative forces a business to think about its history, the personalities involved, their backgrounds, and why the company was started.

What was the bigger picture? Was it about providing a better offering to the market or changing the way a particular product or service was delivered? Alternatively, was the vision to introduce an existing product or service to a new area? Remembering how and why it came into existence can help to articulate the essence of a business. This is not the corporate faceless speak which is routinely regurgitated, but a narrative developed about real people with genuine stories. A good narrative can enhance a company's reputation and demonstrate its authenticity in a way that very few other approaches can achieve.

Today, a business must have clarity about its sense of identity, in order to be able to deliver a consistent message across all the different channels with which it must engage its patrons. These include face to face, on its own website, on blogs, in forums, on other people's websites, on YouTube, on social networks such as Facebook, LinkedIn, Twitter and a plethora of other places that exist.

Today, we live in a 'YouTube World' with unparalleled transparency. Increasingly, in one way or another, everything is recorded and documented. For example, individuals sitting in an audience will tweet what is happening, in real time. Similarly, using just a mobile phone, people have the ability to take pictures or video any sudden occurrence of interest and upload them to Flickr or YouTube. Whether it is expressing a point of view on dedicated areas of a website such as Amazon, disseminating opinions on blogs or providing customer feedback in forums, there are few secrets anymore. In this context, a business that does not know what it stands for is very unlikely to be able to instil enthusiasm in those it wishes to engage.

The internet today gives everyone the potential to have a say and be heard. It connects us in an unprecedented way. Marketing is no longer directed at passive consumers by businesses that can pay to control the flow of information. Today, marketing is conducted less by messaging and more by conversations. Some of these are between companies and customers, but many are between the consumers themselves, without any involvement from the business about which they are speaking.

In the context of a conversation, it is no longer a company's image that is vital. Rather, it is reputation that will determine a business's success. In other words, it is no longer what companies say about themselves that matters; it is what others say that really counts.

- Today, marketing is two-way. Companies can engage directly with consumers, but now customers also have access to a variety of communication channels. This can mean that more material is produced by consumers about a business than by the company itself.

- Consumers are more likely to take notice of what other customers say than any communication from a business. With the plethora of platforms available, this means that conversations in which the company has no part are often taking place.

- Marketing is undertaken less by traditional messaging and more in the context of conversations and discussions. In reality this means that much of a company's marketing will inadvertently be undertaken by others. Consequently, marketing is no longer about the image companies create (what they say) but the reputation that they earn (what others say).

- Customers today are buying experiences, which requires them to make more of an emotional investment. They inadvertently become 'stakeholders' in the business. This results in companies having to reflect the values of their prospects and customers.

- Marketing is part of the experience delivery, not separate from it. Every single interaction with, and message from, a business is part of the experience.

- Today, an increasing number of conversations are taking place within trusted networks and social media. These places require a higher standard of behaviour from companies, an honesty and integrity not required on a billboard or TV commercial.

- By not pretending to have all the answers, companies can encourage engagement and participation from their clientele. Providing consumers with the mechanism to generate feedback and ideas will assist a business in staying vibrant and delivering an experience that is authentic and exciting.

KEY-POINT SUMMARY CONTINUED...

- One aspect that can aid businesses in understanding who they are and engaging with customers is a narrative. This is not faceless corporate speak, but a narrative developed about real people with genuine stories. A good narrative can enhance a company's reputation and demonstrate authenticity.

CHAPTER 09

Controlling to sharing

The creation of the internet, combined with advances in technology, presents both individuals and companies with unprecedented opportunities. At the same time, however, one could argue that the landscape is more competitive than it has ever been, as many barriers to market have come down and, therefore, there are more entities trying to compete.

For example, there were 1,186,900[1] registered companies in the United Kingdom in 1990. By 2009, this had more than doubled to 2,722,700.[2] Similarly, in the United States, registered companies grew by over a million from 6,319,300[3] in 1992 to 7,601,160[4] by 2006. However, this is only a small part of the story. With the collapse of the Berlin Wall and the rise of both India and China, the Western industrial economies now find themselves competing with literally billions of extra people. As technology increasingly renders geographical boundaries irrelevant for many purchases, this competition becomes even more fervent. Of course, the same facts also present companies with fresh and exciting opportunities. These territories provide Western industrialized countries with new markets in which to expand, as growing businesses and an emerging middle class look to purchase goods and services. In this global market, however, it is the very nature of competition and how you respond to it that has really changed.

Before the internet, in most areas of our lives, we had fewer choices. There was far less access to information or communication channels available. This made locating, contacting and ordering from companies further afield extremely difficult. Therefore, people were much more tied to local suppliers when making a purchase. This resulted in businesses, for the most part, competing with a handful of other providers within the geographical territories they covered. If you did not get the business, a competitor you knew well probably would. This world of relative scarcity made business a zero-sum game. It encouraged rivals to compete head on and be obsessed with each other's activities. In this environment, companies tried to protect their ideas by limiting access to them in case they were stolen by the competition.

In the main, businesses tried to keep confidential any fresh ideas involving messaging, strategy, new products or services and promotions. Companies would compete by protecting plans and keeping much of their operations secret. For a few industries, where there are still a small number of participants in the market, this approach *may* still work; in other words, sectors where scarcity still exists and customer choice remains extremely limited. However, most companies no longer operate in this environment.

The changing nature of competition

Today, the very nature of competition has changed. Most companies operate in a marketplace with an abundance of suppliers. When you are competing in a locality with three other rivals, it may make sense to obsess about their activities and go head to head against them. But what happens when three become 3,000 or more? And where the web has enabled the creation of so many mini markets, with whom are you contending anyway? For example, Cafepress,[5] a website which allows individuals to create and sell their own merchandise, has over 6.5 million users. Lemonade,[6] a site which lets people create their own virtual stands, recommending products and services, has over 43,000[7] individual stand owners. So, if you are selling products or services, are you now up against the over 90 million[8] users on eBay? If you are a recruitment agent, are you now trying to compete with Craigslist.com where people from all over the world can outsource jobs?

Scarcity thinking led companies to become controlling, protective and restrictive in allowing access to their goods and services. With few choices available, consumers would often enquire about your offering merely because you were one of the few companies supplying their geographical area. Frequently shouting at people, via the traditional marketing channels, would ensure that prospects knew of your existence when they were looking to make a purchase.

In the mass marketing era, many companies provided very similar products and services. These businesses were often serving an extremely wide demographic in order for the economies of scale to work. This often meant that decidedly similar companies were trying to win business from the same customers. However, we are now operating in the realm of many mini markets. The new world of abundance means that consumers can always find products and services that are more personal to them. They are no longer forced to compromise in their choice of purchase as they did previously. Now, everyone wants to find something to suit them exactly.

The result is that consumers will no longer settle for impersonal mass products when there are more personalized choices available. Companies are now being forced to think of every customer as an individual and respond to their own special requirements, as people are prepared to pay for a more personal experience. Today's consumers are increasingly used to personalizing everything they do, whether it is buying only certain tracks from an album or picking individual subject categories of news streams that are then delivered directly to their inbox. We live in a world of personalization.

As customers find new alternatives that are more appealing to their individual tastes, they develop a greater expectation of this availability in all aspects of their lives. They therefore continue to look for more personal choices. The whole situation then becomes a self-fulfilling prophecy. Technology and the internet perpetuate this situation because they enable personalization to be delivered cost-effectively. Today, businesses can deliver experiences designed just for us, and with us. These circumstances create an environment where many more companies can operate, each serving a very specific type of clientele. The result is that companies that would have been in competition years ago are now increasingly likely to be potential collaborators.

For example, in the early 1990s, two high street accountants, covering a similar area, would have probably been competing for exactly the same clients. Today, if a small accountancy practice wants to thrive it is much better off specializing in certain niche market sectors. So, our two-partner accountancy firm, in earlier chapters, decided to concentrate on small business entrepreneurs. This is where it had a story to tell and specialist expertise it could offer. It is, of course, perfectly possible that both accountants are still competing directly. However, in a working environment comprising lots of mini markets, it is more likely that, although there may be some overlap, each accountant will be working in slightly different domains. If this is the case, there is an opportunity for these accountants to collaborate and pass potential clients to each other. This would have been less likely in the mass market era when both accountants would have been serving a very wide and similar demographic within their locality. In other words, today it is often more sensible to leverage a potential competitor, and work with them, than compete in the traditional way.

The mindset of abundance

In fact, leveraging partnerships with other aligned businesses is vital. It means thinking collaboratively instead of competitively. It is a completely different mindset. The thinking in this approach is the polar opposite of the attitude that comes with scarcity; that is, control and protect. Today, in the majority of markets people have an abundance of choice. Abundance thinking means understanding that, in most cases, trying to protect and control information is futile. If you have had an idea, it is highly likely that someone else has had it as well. Everybody now has the wherewithal to distribute and disseminate content with ease. Therefore, however reticent you are in sharing your ideas, it is probable that they will find their way to market anyway, just via someone else.

Abundance thinking also recognizes that today, trying to control and take ownership of information is often not a sustainable strategy. As soon as an idea is out in the market, the ease with which it can travel and the tools available that give everyone opportunity to comment, manipulate or alter the idea mean that control is not realistic. Abundance thinking, therefore, is about sharing and collaborating. It recognizes that the internet is a fantastic tool for creating opportunities through this very kind of approach.

In the old days of scarcity, knowledge gave you power. A business, therefore, would try and protect this knowledge and use it to draw in customers. The web, however, has made it easy to disseminate knowledge. Consequently, we now have access to it in abundance. There are more ideas available than we could all use in a lifetime. It is no longer having knowledge that gives you power, as it is something to which we all have access. Rather, it is the sharing of knowledge and expertise that gives you the attention of others. In a world where the scarcest resource is customer attention, attracting that attention will lead towards success.

For example, I worked with an association for company chief executives. It had an enormous pool of resources that could be accessed online. However, it was only available for members. At the time, the organization took the view that this fantastic wealth of resources was a member perk and, therefore, should be protected from anyone else. The information was excellent. It contained an array of expertise and knowledge. However, it was unrealistic to think that similar prowess could not be found elsewhere on the internet. While the members of this organization may have appreciated the resources available, I doubt if it was this that either led them to join or retained them. After all, why would people pay for information that could be accessed elsewhere for free?

Meanwhile, consider all the people who, every day, would be searching for this type of expertise on the internet, and could have been using these resources. These potential prospects may have been unaware of the existence of this organization and the value it could offer. By making this information freely available, how many new potential members could the organization have attracted? How many more people would it have actively engaged? How much stronger would this association's reputation and market position have been among its core clientele, chief executives? What considerable word of mouth would this resource have generated?

Scarcity thinking worked when having this information was special. At that time, protecting it, and using it to encourage people to join your organization, made sense. However, in a world of abundance, the real power of this material is in sharing it, not keeping it securely away from public consumption. Today, scarcity thinking will actually prevent you from being competitive, rather than making you more so. Those that do not share knowledge and expertise will find it harder to engage and gain people's attention. Subsequently, they will find themselves bypassed by others that do. In a world of scarcity, protecting knowledge might have led prospects to seek you out. In a world of abundance, it will mean that they will go somewhere else.

The importance of sharing and collaboration

Technology and the internet have made disseminating expertise and cooperating with others easy. Right across the world, we are now seeing the sharing of knowledge, collaborations and discussions taking place in unprecedented ways. Failure to participate will result in a business being left behind. Whether it is on social networks, dedicated forums or blogs etc, or using tools such as e-mail, Skype and instant messaging, it is delusive to think that it is now an option for any company to try to opt out of this trend.

This approach to sharing and collaboration is highlighted by Open Source. That is, communities dedicated to producing all sorts of free products and services by cooperating and working together. This is done on what is called a 'General Public Licence'. This means that anyone can use or alter the platform. The Linux operating system was one of the first of these collaborations to have a large impact. It is a real rival to Microsoft; yet, it has been produced completely by experts and enthusiasts collaborating and giving of their time for nothing. Anyone can use the platform completely free of charge. The internet browser Firefox was created in the same way. It currently has 24.23 per cent of the market.[9] This is market share which potentially could have gone to Microsoft's Internet Explorer, Apple's Safari or Google's

Chrome. Yet, it was not paid for by one large corporation. Rather, it was a collaboration between developers giving of their time for nothing. 'Free' is now competing against some of the biggest companies in the world. Wikipedia is another famous example of mass collaboration in action. It currently accounts for 12.558 per cent[10] of all internet traffic, has 3,186,767 pages[11] and entries in 272 languages.[12] There are few businesses that would have succeeded in building and maintaining such a large resource. However, this is happening right now, by way of mass collaboration and the sharing of knowledge.

In fact, there are examples of companies sharing and collaborating all over the internet, in order to be able to compete. For example, Facebook, Twitter and LinkedIn have opened up their platforms with APIs (application programming interfaces). This enables others to build online businesses and applications that integrate with these companies. This approach helps to keep these social networks relevant, as they are constantly able to offer their users new tools and functionality through third parties. It also helps them to widen their reach, as every business that chooses to integrate with them becomes a de facto referral and free piece of marketing.

Google is another example. In order to challenge the mobile market, Google ensured that its Android operating system was on an open development platform. This makes it easily customizable, enabling programmers to develop all sorts of enhancements. In so doing, Google hopes to be unrivalled in the value it will be able to offer the user. In turn, this could potentially make Google's Android system the most attractive one to consumers. Despite its size and success, Google couldn't hope to achieve this goal without sharing and collaborating with the wider community.

Today, innovation is happening so quickly that it becomes increasingly unlikely that any one company can compete on its own. Therefore, it is imperative that businesses share and collaborate. As the world becomes increasingly complex, and we have more knowledge and choice than ever before, the market becomes more specialized. In order to be able to deliver valued experiences, companies must look to partner with individuals, other businesses and the wider community.

Today, in order to stay relevant, businesses must be creative, innovative and fast. While collaboration and the sharing of ideas help this process, keeping everything under your control and protected actually hinders it.

As long as some businesses are willing to share their ideas and cooperate with others, for example the communities that make up the Open Source movement, then others may have to do likewise. Otherwise, quite simply, companies will be left behind. Wireless technology, together with laptops and next-generation mobile devices, means that collaboration no longer has any boundaries. It can happen almost anywhere, any time. Social platforms now make it relatively easy to identify and connect with relevant people. Meanwhile, the software now available to manage complex workflow means that any barriers to working with others are all but disappearing, for companies of any size.

Sites like eLance.com make it possible to utilize expertise, almost anywhere in the world, in order to achieve particular objectives. Sharing information, across the globe, can be a cost-effective way of accessing some of the best minds available. It is often cheaper now for companies to partner, collaborate, share and leverage human resources and knowledge than ever attempt to undertake tasks internally. Companies that do not embrace this new world order will not be able to compete in the marketplace.

Personalization and the new working environment

The move to personalization also provides opportunities for small businesses to offer niche experiences. This comes at a time when the middle market is disappearing, as consumers increasingly move towards two extremes. In a world of personalization and choice, customers who care about a particular product or service look for a highly personal experience, something special. On the other hand, for the purchases that a particular individual simply deems necessary, the acquisition becomes merely a commodity and, therefore, cost and convenience become the biggest issues in making a decision.

Consequently, we are witnessing the growth of a highly personalized 'premium experience' being offered at one end of the market, and the expansion of 'no frills' offerings at the other. This is having a polarizing effect and making the middle ground untenable.

This comes at a time when no one has a job for life anymore. Consequently, there is an increase in people working for themselves. We are entering the dawn of a new economy. Companies will progressively be smaller entities that come together for projects, to deliver highly personal specific experiences for niche markets, or to work on particular challenges. Consequently, the world of work may start to look more like the film industry, where people work on a film collectively and then go their separate ways.

This way of working is not suited to tight controls and the protection of knowledge. Instead, a mindset embracing openness and transparency will be required. This collaborative approach is vital when trying to deliver experiences rather than products or services. Experiences require an offering that is much more three-dimensional than a traditional product line or service capability. There are many aspects in being able to provide an experience to customers, and that will often mean operating with others to deliver that promise.

For example, take an experience such as a pop concert. It consists of various elements. The artist or band that everyone has come to see is one entity. The set design will be delivered by another company. The sound will be mixed and operated by a further provider, as will the merchandise and food concessions, which are often rented separately. Roadies, who build and dismantle the set in every venue, need to be employed. Meanwhile, the security required will be supplied by others still. In other words, several constituents share, collaborate and come together to deliver an experience. Increasingly, this is a strategy that more traditional businesses will adopt, albeit in a slightly different way.

Customers will also require your business to collaborate with others as they demand seamless integration of the different products and services they use. This may necessitate a company sharing information and ideas with a competitor, in order to ensure that their solutions work together for customers that use both. Partnering could mean that each company attracts more business. Conversely, refusing to work with others could lead to customers looking for alternative suppliers. So, a software supplier offering both customer relationship management and accounting software may find itself working with a provider that offers more popular customer relationship management solutions. Although these companies are technically competitors, without integrating each other's products they risk frustrating customers of both, who, as a result, may go elsewhere.

Co-creation with customers

One of the most effective ways for a business to supply a personalized experience and provide value is by co-creating with customers. However, in order for a company to enable customers to contribute, it has to be willing to share and collaborate. It is almost impossible to facilitate this cooperation while trying to control and protect. Businesses that don't embrace this new paradigm are in danger of missing out. We live in a world where the greatest innovations and value will not necessarily come from inside your business. Customers are posting ideas and opinions all over the internet, which can be seen by everyone. Social networks, forums and the conversations that take place on these platforms are as rich in great new concepts as anything a business can come up with on its own. For example, Idea-a-day.com sends me a free idea every day from one of their fellow subscribers. New thinking is everywhere.

The idea of consumers being actively involved in a company's innovations was predicted as far back as 1981 by Alvin Toffler in his book *The Third Wave*. Coining the word 'prosumer',[13] he described a world where the customer is both the producer and consumer in the creation of the product.

Today, co-creation works because customers want to be involved. The internet is an active not passive medium. It provides everybody with a voice and makes it easier for customers to participate in designing products and services, in order to create their own unique experience. The increasing importance of co-creation, together with user-generated content (where customers provide the content which contributes to the experience of others, eg on YouTube or Amazon reviews), shows that Alvin Toffler's prediction of the prosumer has absolutely come true.

Marketing is now about conversations and engagement, not broadcast and transactions. By its very nature this is a sharing and collaborative process. The scarcest resource today, which companies require, is customer attention. A business that has this has a huge competitive advantage in any given market. Only a company that is willing to open up and share will be able to engage people sufficiently in order to keep their attention.

Once a consumer gives your company their attention, it is important not to lose it. Collaborating with aligned businesses, maybe even ones that you have traditionally seen as a competitor, can help in ensuring that within your area of competence there is nothing with which you cannot assist. This may be delivering a solution yourself, providing some knowledge or expertise via a third party, or even recommending an alternative supplier. Through this cooperation, you become and remain an information hub for your customers. They are then more likely to engage with you and ask your advice again in the future. In other words, you keep their attention. Without collaborating, it is less likely that this will be achieved.

In creating a hub or community with which customers are frequently engaged, you will start to build a good reputation and generate positive word of mouth. This can happen only if you provide value which consumers want to share or talk about. The further your business is willing to go in being open and transparent, the more material will be available to aid this process. The greatest risk to a business today is not sharing and giving information away for free. Rather, it is not doing it and being outsmarted by those that do.

A new age of openness

Openness means that employees should also be encouraged to blog, tweet and use social networks. Too many companies still think in terms of protect and control. With this mentality, the potential for missing out is growing all the time. By being transparent, companies have much less to fear on these social platforms than if they are trying to be guarded and secretive.

It is imperative that companies shift their mindset from control and protection to one of sharing and collaboration. This approach changes the dynamic of a business and provides new opportunities for developing strategic partnerships. In fact, companies should no longer think in terms of customers, suppliers, associates or alliances. Instead, they should think of strategic partnerships where everyone, from a supplier to a customer, is a partner. The two key questions to ask in all these exchanges are: 1) Are you providing value? 2) Are you receiving value?

For example, with customers, are you keeping them engaged? Are you providing knowledge, information and supplying a great experience? In other words, are they getting value? Conversely, you should look at your clients and see which ones give you value. Who recommends you the most? Who spends the most? Who contributes the best ideas? These customers need to be rewarded. More resources and time should be allocated to looking after them than others. This does not mean neglecting any of your clientele. However, every company has finite resources, and more should go to those customers who help make your business increasingly desirable.

Today, smaller companies can compete with some of the world's biggest, by leveraging, partnering and collaborating with others. All businesses, in such a competitive landscape, need to strive to continually get better at what they do. Sharing and collaboration allow for faster innovation with less investment required. All the best companies are now sharing and opening up in order to provide increasing value to their customers.

For example, Amazon encourages its clientele to write reviews. It enables people to become affiliates and receive commission by selling the products that Amazon carries via their own blogs or websites. It also facilitates people in selling their own inventory, by leveraging Amazon's infrastructure. This open approach allows Amazon to offer more value to its own customers, by making a bigger product range available through others. This, in turn, makes it less likely to lose out to a competitor. With this approach, Amazon increases the amount of sales channels it has, while raising marketing awareness. This is all achieved without having to invest very much of its own money. Moreover, all this customer interaction means that Amazon is much more likely to stay up to date with market trends. Partnering and leveraging is a very cost-effective mechanism for penetrating new markets. This is an aspect of business which otherwise is often costly and difficult to undertake on your own.

Quite simply, the more you are willing to open up and share, the greater the scope for engagement. Consequently, you are likely to receive an increase in opportunities coming into your business. Being closed and controlling is scarcity thinking, and, over the long term, will severely damage your business. For example, with the onset of the music file-sharing service, Napster, in 1999[14] the music industry started to fight a battle of trying to protect the copyright of its product. This is a battle in which it has failed miserably. Today, only 5 per cent of all music downloads are paid for.[15] Moreover, one of the companies that has been able to make music downloads a success is Apple.[16] They, of course, are not even a music company but a technology business.

What if the music industry, in 1999, had taken a more open and collaborative approach? Instead of trying to protect copyright, what if the record companies had made their catalogues available on their own websites for free, and then found ways of upselling and monetizing the situation? What would the music industry look like today if companies such as Universal or Sony Music had an engaged subscriber base of millions? They would have an incredible amount of data on every customer. The opportunities for partnering with other businesses, hosting unique events and producing special merchandise, all of which could be made relevant to a specific clientele, are unbelievable. The opportunities seem endless. These are obviously rhetorical questions, but the principle is sound. Today, value has shifted. Companies that made money by controlling and protecting information need to find new ways to create an income from their offering. The internet is a world of sharing and transparency. Opportunities will be developed by embracing this rather than trying to put the genie back in the bottle.

Businesses must understand that the world of digital and the internet have changed the rules. What once worked for companies – protect and control – will now damage them beyond belief. Conversely, what would have been deemed commercial suicide back in the 1990s and before – that of sharing and collaborating on a scale previously unseen – is now the only way that companies can compete in today's business environment.

- We are now operating in a world of many mini markets. Consumers will no longer settle for impersonal mass products when there are more personalized choices available.

- It is no longer having knowledge that gives you power, as knowledge is now something to which we all have access. Rather, today it is the sharing of knowledge and expertise which gives you the attention of others.

- Technology and the internet have made disseminating expertise and cooperating with others easy. Right across the world we are seeing the sharing of knowledge, collaborations and discussions taking place in unprecedented ways. Failure to participate will result in a business being left behind.

- The middle market is disappearing as consumers increasingly move towards two extremes. We are witnessing the growth of a highly personalized premium experience being offered at one end of the market, and the expansion of 'no frills' offerings at the other.

- Companies will progressively be smaller entities that come together for projects, to deliver highly personal specific experiences for niche markets or to work on particular challenges. Consequently, the world of work may start to look more like the film industry where people work on a film collectively and then, when finished, go their separate ways. Thus, a mindset of openness and transparency will be required.

- One of the most effective ways for a business to supply a personalized experience and provide value is co-creating with customers. In order for a company to enable customers to contribute, it has to be willing to share and collaborate. It is almost impossible to facilitate this cooperation while trying to control and protect.

KEY-POINT SUMMARY CONTINUED...

- The greatest risk to a business today is not sharing and giving information away for free. Rather, it is not doing it and being outsmarted by those that do. The more a business is willing to open up and share, the greater the scope for customer engagement.

PART 05

CONCLUSION

CHAPTER 10

It's not about you, it's about the customer

In the old days of mass marketing, companies would pay money to shout at their potential customers. There was a time, however, when consumers would listen to many of these messages.

In the days before digital radio and recording devices, millions of channels and the proliferation of media, people did not have the plethora of ways to screen these advertisements out as they do today.

Before the internet and the access to information that we all now enjoy, many of these messages would provide consumers with potentially interesting information. Now, however, this material is entirely accessible at the point at which people decide they need it. Therefore, people are no longer willing to be shouted at and interrupted at a company's time of choosing.

And this is entirely the point. Where companies proceeded to shout via television, radio, billboards, advertising pages, the phone, the letterbox etc, for most people, most of the time, this advertising was completely out of context and consequently quite an obtrusive interruption. For example, having decided not to take a summer vacation this year, I would then receive a holiday brochure advertising summer destinations to which to take the family. Or, having purchased a brand new car just a few months earlier, I would be bombarded by TV commercials and direct mail literature promoting a particular manufacturer's latest model.

As database programs and customer relationship management packages became more efficient, certain companies, privy to the data, would try to shout at us with more appropriate timing; for example, the mobile phone company that knew when my contract expired, or the insurance provider aware that my policy was up for renewal. While these businesses were the exception rather than the rule, their shouting was, for the most part, relatively unsophisticated. Normally a letter or phone call was sent, with a very transactional approach taken towards the customer. Although the timing was better, it was far from perfect, and still often felt intrusive.

The result would be that I received a call to renew my car insurance while trying to board a train, on the way home from work, or a sales letter was delivered while I was dealing with a myriad of other challenges. Consequently, the letter was put on one side and forgotten about and the phone call was ended abruptly as I asked them to call back another time. They never did.

Why old marketing is too company focused for today

Of course, most companies producing advertising messages were not privy to data of this kind. Therefore, the material was necessarily as much about the company as it was about the customer. The shouting tended to be benefit led, that is, 'this is what we, the company, can do for *you*, the customer'. For example, we (the company) can provide you (the customer) with the most fuel-efficient car, saving you money and running costs. Moreover, with an extended five-year warranty and all features as standard, you will never have been offered such luxury at this price. Now, while this messaging may or may not have been appealing to a particular prospect, the message was as much about the company – *we* have the most fuel-efficient car, *we* offer a five-year warranty, *we* offer all features as standard – as it was about the customer. *You* will save money on running costs, *you* will have more security in the purchase, *you* will have more luxury for your money than has ever been available previously.

Marketers have always aimed to communicate information about a suitable product or service, to an appropriate customer, at the relevant time. The problem, in the days of mass marketing, was that the messaging was necessarily as much about the product or service as it was customer focused. In the main, the 'right customer' could only be identified with what proved to be mostly quite crude demographics. Moreover, except in some exceptional circumstances, timing was often completely unidentifiable.

So, a company may have chosen to market summer holidays in January, February or March, because that is when, historically, people tended to book them. This is, however, fairly crude, and it certainly did not mean that they reached the right prospect at exactly the right moment. Of course, there are many purchases where generalizing about timing is impossible. For the most part, the moment when the acquisition of many business-to-business services and many household items takes place cannot be successfully identified with any precision. A company would have to be privy to some specific insight, regarding particular individuals, in order to know these details.

Conveying relevant messages to the right people, at the most appropriate time, has always been the aim of the marketer. Over the years the mechanisms and approaches for facilitating this outcome have changed as wider developments in society have taken place. Today, the abundance of choice customers have, combined with their easy access to information, means that, once again, marketing has to evolve to reflect these changing circumstances.

Consumers are no longer sitting ducks waiting to be bombarded with marketing messages that are completely out of context and delivered at a time not of their choosing. Today, customers will browse, research and buy at their convenience. In fact, the internet is enabling people to achieve instant gratification and immediate satisfaction in many areas of their lives. The result is that customers tend to search for new products or services almost at the exact point they decide they are required, because the expectation is that they will be readily available.

The new value in immediacy

People are becoming increasingly impatient at having to stand in queues. In fact, consumers are now less tolerant of having to wait for anything at all. The opportunity for a business today is that people are willing to pay more for immediacy. In a world where we are all pushed for time, and impatient, we value speed as never before.

This phenomenon makes timing more important than it has ever been. For example, I am an avid reader. Years ago, I would plan the purchase of a new book. When I was halfway through the volume I was reading, I would, at a convenient time, go into my local store and choose my next publication. It would then be ready for me when my current one was finished. With the advent of the internet, I became less organized. As I came towards the end of a book, I would choose my next read by visiting Amazon, knowing that it could be with me within 24 hours if necessary. Today I do not even do that. On finishing a text, I now visit ebooks.com, browse, download the next one immediately, and start reading straight away.

The changing nature of segmentation

In short, we are moving from a world where *who* is buying is no longer necessarily the most important question. Rather, increasingly, the vital detail is *when* they purchase. In the age of mass marketing, most of the shouting in which companies engaged was out of context. For example, a company would shout at me about its new improved washing powder. At the time, I was neither purchasing any powder nor thinking about doing the washing, but trying to relax with my family after a long and busy day.

In this scenario, the best chance of a business having a well-received message was to make sure that, at the very least, it went to the right person. Companies would try to break the audience down by demographics, such as age, gender, ethnicity, income etc. So, literature advertising a luxury new sports car might be sent to men over 40, and mailed to houses in expensive areas in which to live.

Meanwhile, a perfume created for young women would be advertised during a TV show that they would be expected to watch.

Companies should still have a good idea of the demographic make-up of their customer. However, today, strategies solely based on segmentation such as age, gender, ethnicity, income etc are no longer satisfactory. The increasing proliferation of mobile devices fitted with GPS (global positioning system: a location-based technology) and with access to the internet means that there are a growing number of consumers who can engage with your business at the exact moment they feel it is relevant for them. Today:

- The most important aspect for a company is its ability to solve issues and enhance people's situation, *in the moment.*
- 'When' is as important as 'who'.
- Segmentation is more about customer behaviour than demographics.
- It is all about context.

There are now businesses trying to use new technology, such as GPS, as a broadcast tool; in other words, taking new technology and applying it to the old rules of mass marketing, which is to completely miss the point. For example, I was at an airport not so long ago. Via Bluetooth, I received a message from a newsagent in the terminal. On presenting it with the text it sent to my mobile, I could receive 50 per cent off the price of a newspaper. In reality, this was no more than using new technology as an old-fashioned broadcast mechanism. There really was no context in the message as far as I was concerned, I just happened to be nearby. However, I was neither looking for, nor did I want to purchase, a newspaper. The context, in this case, was not for me but actually for the newsagent. It was all about the newsagent. It wanted me to visit its shop because it knew I was in the vicinity.

Using mobile devices to broadcast to consumers does not seem to present a sustainable long-term opportunity. This is because, if the odd message does work, and it will probably be as much to do with the novelty as anything else, then more companies will want to participate. Imagine a visit to a high street, airport or shopping centre where your mobile device is bombarded with messages. If this were to happen, most of us would try to stop receiving them, or screen them out, as they quickly went from novelty to annoyance. Moreover, the personal nature of a mobile device would make some of us feel that these broadcast messages were offensively obtrusive. Where communications like this could be effective is with point-of-sale displays or to enhance your experience in a particular shop, museum etc. If you were asked at the beginning of your visit whether you wanted to receive this material, you could choose to opt in if you perceived it would add value.

The power of context

In reality, the power of context, like all aspects of new marketing, is that it should be completely consumer led. It should not be the case that marketers use mobile devices as a way of trying to reach people all the time. On the other hand, people can now reach marketing at all times. Today, customers have the opportunity to engage with any business at exactly the moment, and in the place, they want the interaction to happen. Whatever the situation, prospects will look to communicate with a business at the very moment they feel it is relevant for them. This could be when they are killing time at a railway station or in an airport lounge, when sitting comfortably at home or when walking down the high street near the particular shop with which they wish to interact.

Previously, when businesses shouted at consumers in order to communicate, the messages were necessarily as much about the company as they were about the customer. There was little value in the actual material, except the occasional imparting of some information. Rather, a company would shout at a prospect, telling them what value they could receive if they were to make a purchase.

Increasingly, shouting is becoming less effective as a way of communicating a message. Instead, businesses require prospects to approach them. There is only one reason, however, for people to access marketing and engage with a company. It is because the marketing and communications provide value in the particular context in which a person chooses to interact.

Thus, marketing is no longer about you at all. It is completely about the customer. The only way for marketing to engage and, therefore, ultimately be successful is to provide value to the customer in their particular situation.

The result is that marketing is no longer a means to an end. It provides an experience, on its own merit, by adding value to the context and situation in which a particular person decides to interact. In other words, 'sticky marketing' is not solely about the product, service or experience you provide. It is an experience, product or service in its own right; or as Steve Jones so aptly identified, 'It's got nothing to do with music, you silly cow!'

Moreover, as products and services become completely commoditized, the value and differentiation that customers receive are in the experience provided, rather than the tangible goods or services themselves. This, in turn, makes the 'when' of a purchase significant in a way it perhaps has never been. As digital technology increasingly permeates our everyday lives, this has a huge significance for marketers.

For example, while out with friends, we may access the internet or an iPhone application such as 'Around Me',[1] providing details of available cafés and restaurants, clubs and bars, in order to decide what to do next. Meanwhile, 'augmented reality' applications, whereby digital images can be superimposed on real streets and displays at which we are currently looking, can be accessed to enhance a current situation in which we find ourselves.

Thus, while it has always been true that a certain degree of purchasing has been triggered by events, our ability to access information inside these situations has now been enhanced. This means that an increasing amount of purchasing will be triggered within the moment. The result is that, in order to be effective, marketing has to be increasingly contextual. Marketers are going to have to be much more conscious about when and where someone is, when they want to engage. This will be more important, and create more opportunities, for a business than just focusing on who the person is.

For example, a fast food hamburger company might not have wanted to invest in expensive broadcast media in order to market to a high net worth business person. After all, it might not have deemed that individual as part of its target audience. However, if it is raining and a business person is running late for a meeting and feeling hungry, they might very well, at that moment, choose to engage with a fast food hamburger restaurant that offers drive-in facilities. It could be them browsing the internet for their nearest provider, rather than a young family who are demographically more in line with the restaurant's core market.

We are seeing context becoming more relevant in all aspects of our lives. For example, many online networks, including LinkedIn and Facebook, allow for real-time updates, so people can inform others of what they are doing, in the moment. It was Twitter that really kick-started this real-time revolution. Similarly, we are seeing the growing emergence and importance of location-based networks, such as Foursquare,[2] where members tell friends and followers where they are currently.

Behavioural targeting

Today, far more important for marketers than any demographics is behavioural targeting. That is, understanding the context, situation and ways potential customers like to engage with your type of offering. Of course, if businesses get this right, it gives them the opportunity to become closer to their customers and create more value for them. In turn, this allows the growth of a variety of different revenue streams.

A very simple contextual upsell is Amazon's. When you go to click and buy a particular book or album it will immediately recommend some other titles, within the same genre, that others who made your purchase also bought. This uses social proof, which is a very powerful influencer, by showing 'what other people like you' purchased. These recommendations are also provided within the context of an acquisition you are already making. Thus, they add value within your situation, in the moment.

If you run a pizza takeaway, or a nightclub, when do most people look for information about your service? Is it when they are at work on a Friday morning or in the high street on a Saturday night? Should the messaging change according to the time of day? On the Saturday night it is possible that people are looking for somewhere to go right now, whereas, on a Friday morning, it is more likely that someone is browsing for the different options available over the weekend. Given that these circumstances are different, should the way that a company tries to add value to the situation also change?

Similarly, if you sell business-to-business services, when do people access your information? Depending on the time of day, are they at work, at home or on the train travelling to the office? Are they researching an expensive solution? If so, what information would provide value within that context? Alternatively, are they trying to make a quick transaction? How can this experience be made sufficiently easy? Today, it is not just the product or service and demographic of your customer that matter. The context in which somebody engages with your business is vital. It allows you to provide added value, in the moment, and therefore deliver a great experience. In turn, this will make an eventual purchase more likely. It also increases the chances that a customer will want to continue the engagement with your business.

Being able to understand the behaviour of consumers, and the context in which they access particular marketing and information, will also allow companies to offer different solutions to the same customer, depending on their situation. This is because people's preferences change, depending on the context of the purchase they are making.

For example, a business owner, when travelling for work, may look to fly business class. This enables them to check in as late as possible. It makes it easier to sleep and work on the plane, and arrive at their destination relatively fresh and relaxed. When it comes to choosing a hotel, however, they normally select something basic. This is because they spend very little time there and therefore cannot justify the cost of anything more. However, when booking a holiday, this same person has very different criteria. They decide that business class is too expensive and unnecessary. However, they always choose to stay in a much better hotel for their two-week holiday, where there are plenty of facilities and where they can relax. Thus, where demographics may prove to be quite unhelpful in defining the right solution for a customer, context would be much more revealing in understanding the solution for which they are looking.

Understanding consumer behaviour, and the context in which they choose to access your marketing, is vital in being able to provide value. For many businesses, customers will choose to access their communications when they are in the moment and/or area. So, a bar/restaurant may find that many people access its information when they are in the vicinity. This is the power, for example, of geographically based applications on mobile phones, whereby customers can access real-time information, in the moment.

The point is that, today, consumers will decide to access your marketing at their time of choosing. In order to be effective, any communication should make perfect sense to the person, in the context of what they are doing. It should provide value by making them laugh or think or by assisting them in some way. Context, however, does not solely have to be about geographical destinations, that is, where people are physically. Companies can provide value, online, by understanding customer behaviour and using that learning.

Making use of context on the internet

For example, many companies' main online presence is through their website. This usually contains all the information they wish to provide to prospects and customers alike. In other words, businesses have created destinations which they then require people to visit. However, it can be far more powerful for companies to go where their customers are already. So, if many of your customers look for business information on their local Chamber of Commerce web portal, or a particular industry association site, why not offer to provide valuable content for those? In other words, engage with clients within their own context, rather than trying to get them to change their behaviour and come to you, which is a far harder task.

When placing information on the websites and platforms of other companies, it is important to understand what you are trying to achieve. Context is not about delivering your message. Rather, it is about providing value, within the situation in which someone accesses your content. By understanding context, a company can create value, in the moment. In this way, consumers will feel it is worthwhile engaging with you.

For example, a clothes retailer could provide top tips on how to dress to impress, which might feature on a dating website. Alternatively, a recruitment firm could produce an informative tip sheet on interview techniques for a management portal. Value, in the first instance, is not produced through your actual products or services. Rather, it is created by relating your offering to what your customers are looking to achieve. Marketing is no longer a means to an end. It is an end in itself. By developing something greater than just the products or services you offer, you will begin to turn your business into an experience provider. In a world where products and services are commodities, it is this experience that starts to make you attractive.

Social media

One place where companies need to create value around their products and services, if they want to participate, is on social platforms. Numerous businesses are desperate to get involved in social media. This is because it is where many of their customers are spending much of their time. Platforms such as Facebook are increasingly where people are operating many of their social activities. This can be anything from organizing nights out to having conversations and seeing what other friends are doing. Business platforms such as LinkedIn provide opportunities to keep up to date with contacts, make new associations and learn from others. For a company to venture into social media successfully, they must find a way to create real value within the context in which people are operating. However, treating these portals as another broadcast tool is obtrusive in a way that most people will not tolerate. The wrong type of involvement could potentially have an adverse effect on your business.

Companies need to ask themselves three questions in order to ensure they understand context:

1 In what activity are my customers engaged? Are they in conversation with friends, asking for business advice or out for a Saturday night?
2 Where are they? Are they sitting at work or at home, are they standing in the high street or are they on a train or waiting in an airport lounge?
3 How is my content relevant? How does my content/information fit with their current situation? Does it enhance their situation and therefore add real value?

With customers being able to access marketing anywhere and at any time, it is they who have ultimate control. We are now moving from the idea of customer relationship management (CRM) to customer managed relationships (CMR). In other words, customers decide on how, and on what terms, they engage with your business. By enhancing their current situation, you make it much more likely that customers will want to engage with your business. The more you understand consumer behaviour, the easier it becomes to deliver something of real value, in the right context. This is especially true online. By analysing what visitors look at, read, engage with, access and ignore, it becomes easier to understand what they want.

For example, search engines can help you understand how people perceive your products or services, by revealing what language they use to look for them. Programs like Google Trends allow you to analyse the volume with which people use various search terms, within different locations. Context in the online world has often revolved around companies creating targeted advertisements. These are based on a person's search or browsing behaviour. Of course, although this is still a broadcast model of marketing, there is a relevance to the advertisement. Therefore, it is much more likely to be well received by a potential customer. However, as the internet develops, and as we have more knowledge about what the user is doing, it will be possible to deliver much more value than just a targeted advertisement, which many internet users already find obtrusive.

As more of us access information on mobile devices, rather than sitting at home or work, we will, where appropriate, want the internet to provide relevance to our current situation and location. As context becomes increasingly important, marketing communications must take this into consideration. Advertising, wherever it is placed, is normally very transactional in nature. If we now require prospects and customers to access our marketing, at their convenience, we must be thinking about how we engage. This requires that the marketing itself imparts value. It can no longer be only a means to convey the advantages of our products and services.

The growing importance of context also means that the channel used to communicate now has greater significance. In a world of abundance of choice, we are used to being able to obtain products and services at any time and in any place. Today, in so many areas of life, we are no longer constrained by time, space or geographical boundaries. Today, people want to be able to access your offering and information at a time of their choosing.

This view is supported in research undertaken by Blueview Group. Its survey showed that 66 per cent of people base purchasing decisions on the communication channels on offer.[3] Moreover, 61 per cent of people will switch from a company that they already use, to a competitor, if the former could not offer them the channel of communication they desire.[3] Offering multiple channels of communication can often be achieved at negligible cost to a business. However, it allows a company to extend its reach to customers with whom it would not be able to engage in any other way.

Companies that still see marketing as merely transactional will miss opportunities. They will find it increasingly difficult to engage with clients and prospects in the new landscape in which we find ourselves. Marketing is no longer tactical, solely based on short-term campaign ideas for increasing revenue. Now it must be strategic; that is, customer orientated and focused on value creation and long-term engagement. By concentrating on these aspects and evaluating ROE (return on engagement) rather than the traditional ROI (return on investment), businesses will prosper over the long term.

Being able to add value depends on the context in which a person engages with your business. Therefore, in order to achieve this, marketers need to ask themselves *when* a customer accesses their marketing as much as *who* that customer is. In so doing, marketers will start to be able to deliver an experience, and engage with prospects and customers alike, over the long term. There is an exciting future ahead. Marketers now have the opportunity to create long-term value for a business in new and interesting ways.

'Sticky marketing' means understanding that marketing is no longer a means to an end, it is the end in itself.

- The internet is enabling people to achieve instant gratification and immediate satisfaction in many areas of their lives. It is because of this that people are willing to pay more for immediacy. In a world where we are all impatient and pushed for time, we value speed as never before.

- Who is buying is no longer necessarily the most important question. Rather, increasingly, the vital detail is when they purchase. Thus segmentation based solely on demographics such as age, gender, ethnicity, income etc is no longer satisfactory. It therefore becomes more about customer behaviour than demographics.

- With the ubiquity of mobile devices, people can now reach marketing at all times. Customers have the opportunity to engage with any business at exactly the moment, and in the place, they want the interaction to happen. The only way for marketing to engage, therefore, is to provide value to the customer, in their particular situation, and become increasingly contextual.

- Through their website, businesses have created destinations which they require people to visit. However, it can be far more powerful for companies to go where their customers are already. For example, this can mean interacting on certain social platforms or particular industry-specific sites.

- Value, in the first instance, is not produced through a company's actual products or services. It is created by relating a business's offering to what the customer is looking to achieve. In other words, marketing is no longer a means to an end. It is an end in itself.

What the Sex Pistols taught me about marketing

[1] More information about Paul Mex, record producer, can be found at: **www.paulmex.co.uk**.

Chapter 01

[1] Australian politics. Bill Jefferson Clinton, 42nd President of the United States. Excerpt from full text 'The Struggle for the Soul of the 21st Century', BBC, The Dimbleby Lecture 2001, broadcast 14 December 2001 [accessed 1 February 2010]:

> *'Very briefly, what are the main benefits of the modern world? The global economy; it's lifted more people out of poverty in the last twenty years than at any time in history. It's been great for Europe and the United States, in the last few years I was President. It led to huge declines in poverty even as more people were getting rich. Second, the information technology revolution: when I became President in 1993, there were only fifty sites on the worldwide web – unbelievable – fifty. When I left office, the number was three hundred and fifty million and rising. Even before the anthrax scare, there were thirty times as many messages delivered by email as by the postal service in the United States.'*
>
> [online] **http://australianpolitics.com/news/2001/01-12-14.shtml**

[2] Absolute Astronomy. Exploring the Universe of Knowledge. Yellow Pages Overview [accessed 1 February 2010]:

> *'The name and concept of "Yellow Pages" came about in 1883, when a printer in Cheyenne, Wyoming working on a regular telephone directory ran out of white paper and used yellow paper instead. In 1886 Reuben H. Donnelley created the first official yellow pages directory, inventing an industry... Studies by independent companies such as Nielson and*

comScore have shown that Internet Yellow Pages have a very slim percentage of total Internet searches. The majority, over 85% of all Internet searches, occur on the major search engines Google, Yahoo and MSN.'

[online] **http://www.absoluteastronomy.com/topics/ Yellow_Pages#encyclopedia**

[3] Yell. About Yell. Yell UK [accessed 1 February 2010]:

'Yell began life in 1966 as a "Yellow Pages" section in the Brighton telephone directory. Yellow Pages, as part of BT, grew to become the UK's leading provider of classified directory advertising and associated services. In April 2000 the Yellow Pages division of BT became Yell and in June 2001 Yell was purchased from BT by a consortium of private equity investors. In July 2003 Yell was listed on the London Stock Exchange and became Yell Group plc.'

[online] **http://www.yellgroup.com/english/aboutyell-yelluk**

[4] Google. Google Corporate Information. Google Milestones [accessed 1 February 2010]:

'Our company has packed a lot in to a relatively young life. We've captured some of the key milestones in Google's development... August 1998: Sun co-founder Andy Bechtolsheim writes a cheque for $100,000 to an entity that doesn't exist yet: a company called Google Inc. September 1998: Google sets up workspace in Susan Wojcicki's garage at 232 Santa Margarita, Menlo Park.'

[online] **http://www.google.com/corporate/history.html**

[5] DMGT. Daily Mail and General Trust Plc. Media Centre. Acquisition of *Loot*. Posted Friday 17 August 2001 [accessed 1 February 2010]:

'Loot was founded in 1984 and launched its first publication, the London edition of Loot, in 1985.'

[online] **http://www.dmgt.co.uk/mediacentre/ newsreleases/20010817/3236/**

[6] eBay. Who we are. History Timeline [accessed 1 February 2010]:

'On Labor Day weekend in 1995, computer programmer Pierre Omidyar wrote the code for what he called an "experiment": What would happen if everyone in the world had equal access to a single global marketplace? Pierre tested his new auction website by posting a broken laser pointer, which he was about to throw away. And to his

surprise, a collector bought it for $14.83. The sale of a broken laser pointer was the beginning of a radical transformation in commerce.'

[online] **http://www.ebayinc.com/list/milestones**

[7] PC Pro. Latest News. Skype becomes biggest international call carrier. Posted on 20 Jan 2010 at 07:30 [accessed 1 February 2010]:

'Users wanting to call home from abroad are increasingly turning to Skype to the detriment of international carriers, new data reveals. "Skype is now the largest provider of cross-border communications in the world, by far," claims Stephan Beckert, analyst at research firm TeleGeography… Skype's technology allows consumers to make cheap long-distance calls over the internet. It is mostly used on desktops but Skype has made the move into mobile too and it now comes pre-installed on some mobile handsets. According to the firm's data, over the past 25 years, international call volume from telephones has grown at a compounded annual rate of 15%. In the past two years this growth has slowed to only 8%, rising from 376 billion minutes in 2008 to an estimated 406 billion minutes last year. By comparison, Skype's on-net international traffic between two Skype users grew 51% in 2008, and is projected to grow 63% in 2009, to 54 billion minutes. "The volume of traffic routed via Skype is tremendous," says Beckert. "Demand for international voice has been remarkably robust, but it's clearly not recession-proof." Established in 2003 and based in Luxembourg, privately owned Skype has more than 520 million registered customers who use the free web service for voice, video or text communication.'

[online] **http://www.pcpro.co.uk/news/broadband/354928/ skype-becomes-biggest-international-call-carrier**

[8] World Wide Web Consortium. 10th Anniversary. Pre W3C Web and Internet Background [accessed 1 February 2010]:

'End 1990: Development begins for first browser (called "WorldWideWeb"), editor, server, and line-mode browser. Culminates in first Web client–server communication over Internet in December 1990.'

[online] **http://www.w3.org/2005/01/timelines/timeline-2500x998.png**

[9] British Library. Treasures in Full. Gutenberg Bible [accessed 1 February 2010]:

'Printing was one of the most important technical advances in history. It was invented by Johann Gutenberg, a German from Mainz, in the 1450s. An account of his life can be found on this website.

Much earlier, books such as the Diamond Sutra had been produced in China and Korea with type made first of wood and later of bronze. Gutenberg's invention was different: it was possible to print many copies of the same text speedily. It had great commercial potential, but it did not make Gutenberg a rich man.'

[online] **http://www.bl.uk/treasures/gutenberg/background.html**

[10a] The History of Film. Written by Tim Dirks. Film History Before 1920. Part 2 [accessed 1 February 2010]:

'The first public test and demonstration of the Lumieres' camera-projector system (the Cinematographe) was made on March 22, 1895, in the Lumieres' basement. They caused a sensation with their first film, Workers Leaving the Lumiere Factory (La Sortie des Ouviers de L'Usine Lumiere a Lyon), although it only consisted of an everyday outdoor image – factory workers leaving the Lumiere factory gate for home or for a lunch break. As generally acknowledged, cinema (a word derived from Cinematographe) was born on December 28, 1895, in Paris, France. The Lumieres presented the first commercial exhibition of a projected motion picture to a paying public in the world's first movie theatre – in the Salon Indien, at the Grand Cafe on Paris' Boulevard des Capucines. The 20-minute program included ten short films with twenty showings a day.'

[online] **http://www.filmsite.org/pre20sintro2.html**

[10b] PBS. People and Discoveries. KDKA begins to broadcast. 1920 (USA) [accessed 1 February 2010]:

'In 1920, Westinghouse, one of the leading radio manufacturers, had an idea for selling more radios: It would offer programming. Radio began as a one-to-one method of communication, so this was a novel idea. Dr. Frank Conrad was a Pittsburgh area ham operator with lots of connections. He frequently played records over the airwaves for the benefit of his friends. This was just the sort of thing Westinghouse had in mind, and it asked Conrad to help set up a regularly transmitting station in Pittsburgh. On November 2, 1920, station KDKA made the nation's first commercial broadcast (a term coined by Conrad himself). They chose that date because it was election day, and the power of radio was proven when people could hear the results of the Harding–

Cox presidential race before they read about it in the newspaper. KDKA was a huge hit, inspiring other companies to take up broadcasting. In four years there were 600 commercial stations around the country. To keep up with the cost of improving equipment and paying for performers, stations turned to advertisers. In August 1922, the first radio ad, for a real estate developer, was aired in New York City. Networks of local stations developed to share programming and became big business. In 1926, RCA (Radio Corporation of America) formed the first national network, called NBC (National Broadcasting Company). Their first nationwide broadcast was the 1927 Rose Bowl football game from Pasadena. The burgeoning industry made the airwaves so jammed and chaotic that the Federal Radio Commission was established in 1927 to assign frequencies to broadcasters.'

[online] **http://www.pbs.org/wgbh/aso/databank/entries/dt20ra.html**

[10c] BBC. History of the BBC. The BBC Story. 1930s. BBC TV [accessed 1 February 2010]:

'The world's first regular TV service. John Logie Baird had given the first public demonstration of low-definition television back in 1925. There had been experimental transmissions from a studio in Broadcasting House since 1932. On 2 November 1936 the BBC opened the world's first regular service of high-definition television from Alexandra Palace in North London, known affectionately as "Ally Pally".'

[online] **http://www.bbc.co.uk/historyofthebbc/resources/**
factsheets/1930s.pdf

[11] BBC. BBC Sport.What are tennis racquets made of? [accessed 1 February 2010]:

'Racquet frames were made of wood until the 1970s. Now, they're made of graphite, fibreglass and other man-made materials. It means racquets are a lot lighter – but just as strong. Tennis legend Bjorn Borg won 11 Grand Slam titles in the 1970s and 80s using a wooden racquet. In 1991 he made a comeback wanting to prove his old-fashioned wooden racquet was still good enough. But he was blown away by little-known Jordi Arresse using a modern graphite racquet. When big hitter Mark Philippoussis compared the speed of his serves using wood and graphite racquets, they were found to be almost the same. The difference was that the graphite racquet was far more accurate.'

[online] **http://news.bbc.co.uk/sportacademy/hi/sa/tennis/features/**
newsid_3000000/3000836.stm

[12] Brian Wilson. Musicians on Brian. Paul McCartney [accessed 1 February 2010]:

> 'It was Pet Sounds that blew me out of the water. I love the album so much. I've just bought my kids each a copy of it for their education in life... I figure no one is educated musically 'til they've heard that album... I love the orchestra, the arrangements... it may be going overboard to say it's the classic of the century... but to me, it certainly is a total, classic record that is unbeatable in many ways... I've often played Pet Sounds and cried. I played it to John so much that it would be difficult for him to escape the influence... it was the record of the time. The thing that really made me sit up and take notice was the bass lines... and also, putting melodies in the bass line. That I think was probably the big influence that set me thinking when we recorded "Pepper", it set me off on a period I had then for a couple of years of nearly always writing quite melodic bass lines.'
>
> [online] **http://www.brianwilson.com/brian/musicians.html**

[13] Guardian. Technology Blog. Posted by Kevin Anderson. Wednesday 21 January 2009 16.53 GMT [accessed 1 February 2010]:

> 'Facebook meets TV, literally. CNN integrated Facebook with a live video stream of their coverage of Barack Obama's inauguration. This might just jump start more social video experiments... CNN.com said it has served more than 21.3m live video streams, including 1.3m simultaneous streams before Obama gave his address, according to CNET.com. Facebook had 1.5m inauguration-related updates, and Facebook provided these figures:
> - 600,000 status updates have been posted so far through the CNN. com Live Facebook feed
> - There were an average of 4,000 status updates every minute during the broadcast
> - There were 8,500 status updates the minute Obama began his speech.'
>
> [online] **http://www.guardian.co.uk/technology/blog/2009/jan/21/ barackobama-television**

[14] History. This Day in History. General Interest. March 25, 1957. Common Market founded [accessed 1 February 2010]:

> 'On March 25, 1957, France, West Germany, Italy, the Netherlands, Belgium, and Luxembourg sign a treaty in Rome establishing the

European Economic Community (EEC), also known as the Common Market. The EEC, which came into operation in January 1958, was a major step in Europe's movement toward economic and political union… In early 1990s, the European Community became the basis for the European Union (EU), which was established in 1993 following ratification of the Maastricht Treaty.'

[online] **http://www.history.com/this-day-in-history. do?action=Article&id=6847**

[15] Time. Archive: Freedom! The Berlin Wall. Monday, Nov. 20, 1989 [accessed 7 February 2010]:

'For 28 years it had stood as the symbol of the division of Europe and the world, of Communist suppression, of the xenophobia of a regime that had to lock its people in lest they be tempted by another, freer life – the Berlin Wall, that hideous, 28-mile-long scar through the heart of a once proud European capital, not to mention the soul of a people. And then – poof! – it was gone. Not physically, at least yet, but gone as an effective barrier between East and West, opened in one unthinkable, stunning stroke to people it had kept apart for more than a generation. It was one of those rare times when the tectonic plates of history shift beneath men's feet, and nothing after is quite the same.

What happened in Berlin last week was a combination of the fall of the Bastille and a New Year's Eve blowout, of revolution and celebration. At the stroke of midnight on Nov. 9, a date that not only Germans would remember, thousands who had gathered on both sides of the Wall let out a roar and started going through it, as well as up and over. West Berliners pulled East Berliners to the top of the barrier along which in years past many an East German had been shot while trying to escape; at times the Wall almost disappeared beneath waves of humanity. They tooted trumpets and danced on the top. They brought out hammers and chisels and whacked away at the hated symbol of imprisonment, knocking loose chunks of concrete and waving them triumphantly before television cameras. They spilled out into the streets of West Berlin for a champagne-spraying, horn-honking bash that continued well past dawn, into the following day and then another dawn. As the daily BZ would headline: BERLIN IS BERLIN AGAIN.'

[online] **http://www.time.com/time/magazine/ article/0,9171,959058,00.html**

[16] Business Week. Special Report November 5, 2009, 10:07AM EST. Fall of the Berlin Wall: A Victory for Europe. By Gabriele Suder [accessed 1 February 2010]:

> 'Two decades after the collapse of the Iron Curtain, Europe and the world have gained enormously from democratic and economic integration.
>
> … Trade Boost. For business, far-reaching changes in the global economic environment kicked off at that time: The transition to market-based economies in most Central and Eastern European countries created significant opportunities for markets, resources, supplies, and manufacturing. We saw a huge increase in cross-border trade and foreign direct investment, including in services. Almost simultaneously, the emergence of the digital revolution brought with it a decrease in international transaction costs and led to offshore service advantages. Innovations in both developed and developing countries and the emergence of the Asian tigers and the BRIC countries – Brazil, Russia, India, and China – increased the speed of product life cycles and market opportunities, with accelerating globalization taking hold of our economies. Companies turned to cross-border mergers and acquisitions in an effort to improve their global competitiveness, boosting multinational activity in locations until then untouched by market capitalism. From an EU business standpoint, the fall of the Berlin Wall brought a revolution of a unique kind. German reunification expanded the common market in size and population; now, thanks to EU enlargements in 2004 and 2007, the market encompasses 500 million people, with yet more set to join in future years. Indeed, it could be argued that the fall of the Berlin Wall set in motion steps that have solidified Europe's position in international affairs.'
>
> [online] **http://www.businessweek.com/globalbiz/content/nov2009/ gb2009115_371357_page_2.htm**

Chapter 02

[1] World Wide Web Consortium, 10th Anniversary. Pre W3C Web and Internet Background [accessed 1 February 2010]:

> 'End 1990: Development begins for first browser (called "WorldWideWeb"), editor, server, and line-mode browser.

Culminates in first Web client–server communication over Internet in December 1990.'

[online] **http://www.w3.org/2005/01/timelines/timeline-2500x998.png**

[2] SKY TV Timeline [accessed 1 February 2010]:

'1989 Sky launches a "Direct to Home" satellite television service via the Astra satellite with four free-to-air channels including Sky News, Europe's first 24-hour news channel. 1990 Sky and rival broadcaster BSB agree to merge and form BSkyB. Sky Movies uses encryption technology to become a subscription service.'

[online] **http://corporate.sky.com/about_sky/timeline.htm**

[3] Parliament. Liberalization of Aviation in the EU Select Committee on European Union Seventeenth Report [accessed 1 February 2010]:

'14. Within the European Community, the liberalization process began in 1987 with the adoption of a first package of measures aimed at opening up the traditionally restrictive bilateral arrangements. A second package agreed in June 1990 built on this foundation, and a third package of measures was agreed in June 1992. As a result, a single market in air transport in the European Community came into being on 1 January 1993.'

[online] **http://www.publications.parliament.uk/pa/ld200203/ldselect/ ldeucom/92/9203.htm**

[4] EasyJet. First Flight: Key events in our history [accessed 1 February 2010]:

'March 1995: easyJet incorporated to offer low-cost scheduled air services within Europe.

October 1995: The first booking taken on 23 October, as the easyJet telephone reservation centre opens at easyLand, the home of easyJet at London Luton Airport.

November 1995: Inaugural flights from London Luton to Edinburgh and Glasgow, supported by advertising campaign "Making flying as affordable as a pair of jeans – £29 one way". At this time, the airline had two leased Boeing 737-200 aircraft and essentially acted as a "virtual airline" which contracted in everything from pilots to check-in staff.'

[online] **http://www.easyjet.com/EN/About/Information/ infopack_keyevents.html**

[5]   Ryanair. About Us. History of Ryanair [accessed 1 February 2010]:

'1986: Ryanair obtains permission from the regulatory authorities to challenge the British Airways and Aer Lingus' high fare duopoly on the Dublin–London route. Services are launched with two (46-seater) turbo prop BAE748 aircraft. The first flights operate in May from Dublin to London Luton. The launch fare of £99 return is less than half the price of the BA/Aer Lingus lowest return fare of £209. Both British Airways and Aer Lingus slash their high prices in response to Ryanair's. Ryanair starts the first fare war in Europe. With two routes in operation, Ryanair carries 82,000 passengers in its first full year in operation.'

[online] **http://www.ryanair.com/site/EN/about.php**

[6]   The Independent. Mercury available from any telephone. Mary Fagan. Friday, 1 October 1993 [accessed 1 February 2010]:

'Although Mercury has more than 10 per cent of the telecommunications market by revenue, it has made limited inroads into the residential sector. Almost 500,000 households are connected to Mercury via BT local lines and about 200,000 through cable television companies. This compares with a total of 20 million residential customers in the United Kingdom.'

[online] **http://www.independent.co.uk/news/uk/
mercury-available-from-any-telephone-1507928.html**

[7]   Ofgem. Deregulation of supply markets [accessed 1 February 2010]:

'Gas industry privatized – 1986

Electricity industry privatized – 1989

Full competition in gas – 1998

Full competition in electricity – 1999.'

[online] **http://www.ofgem.gov.uk/Markets/Archive/Deregulation%20
of%20supply%20markets%20-%20slides%2026%2011.pdf**

[8]   OpenLearn. Learning Space.1 Exploration of debt.1.3 Liberalisation in the financial services industry [accessed 22 June 2010]:

'…there are other aspects of the social and economic context relevant to understanding debt. One of the most important is the liberalisation of the UK financial services industry. This process has brought about great change within financial services, dating back to legislation passed in the 1980s. This included the Financial Services Act 1986, the Building

Societies Act 1986, and the Banking Act 1987. Together with policy changes by lenders, these acts prompted the diversification by financial institutions into various new activities; relaxed rules on the use by lenders of borrowing from other financial institutions in the world's financial markets to finance their personal lending, and encouraged greater price competition among lenders.'

[online] **http://openlearn.open.ac.uk/mod/resource/ view.php?id=282487**

[9] Mobile Operators Association (MOA). Mobile Phone Usage 1990 [accessed 1 February 2010]:

'Mobile Phone Subscribers: 1990 = 1.14m.'

[online] **http://www.mobilemastinfo.com/information/history.htm**

[10] Optimum Population Trust. UK Population 1990 [accessed 1 February 2010]:

'UK Population mid 1990 = 57.561m.'

[online] **http://www.optimumpopulation.org/ opt.more.ukpoptable.html**

[11] New Scientist. Tech. The pioneering messages made possible by technology (part 2) 12:40 16 October 2008 by Colin Barras. First text message [accessed 1 February 2010]:

'"Merry Christmas" texted Neil Papworth of Sema Group to Richard Jarvis of Vodafone on 3rd December 1992. Papworth actually sent the message from a PC. Riku Pihkonen of Nokia claims to be the first to have physically "texted" from a phone, in 1993.'

[online] **http://www.newscientist.com/article/dn14958-the- pioneering-messages-made-possible-by-technology-part-2.html**

[12a] Guardian. Technology. Series. The internet at 40. Forty years of the internet: how the world changed for ever. Oliver Burkeman. The Guardian, Friday 23 October 2009 [accessed 1 February 2010]:

'In October 1969, a student typed "LO" on a computer... The spread of the internet across the Atlantic, through academia and eventually to the public, is a tale too intricate to recount here, though it bears mentioning that British Telecom and the British government didn't really want the internet at all: along with other European governments, they were in favour of a different networking technology, Open Systems Interconnect. Nevertheless, by July 1992, an Essex-born businessman

named Cliff Stanford had opened Demon Internet, Britain's first
commercial internet service provider. Officially, the public still wasn't
meant to be connecting to the internet. "But it was never a real
problem", Stanford says today. "The people trying to enforce that
weren't working very hard to make it happen, and the people working
to do the opposite were working much harder." The French consulate
in London was an early customer, paying Demon £10 a month instead
of thousands of pounds to lease a private line to Paris from BT.

    After a year or so, Demon had between 2,000 and 3,000 users, but
they weren't always clear why they had signed up: it was as if they had
sensed the direction of the future, in some inchoate fashion, but hadn't
thought things through any further than that. "The question we always
got was: 'OK, I'm connected – what do I do now?'", Stanford recalls. "It
was one of the most common questions on our support line. We would
answer with 'Well, what do you want to do? Do you want to send an
email?' 'Well, I don't know anyone with an email address.'" People got
connected, but they didn't know what was meant to happen next.'

[online] **http://www.guardian.co.uk/technology/2009/oct/23/
internet-40-history-arpanet**

[12b] Living Internet. Email History: Dave Crocker. AOL [accessed 1 February
2010]:

'Online Services. In 1993, the large network service providers America
Online and Delphi started to connect their proprietary email systems to
the Internet, beginning the large scale adoption of Internet email as a
global standard.'

[online] **http://www.livinginternet.com/e/ei.htm**

[13] Barb. Since 1981. Top 10 Programmes

BARB Top 10 UK TV Programmes 1990 [accessed 18 February 2010]:
Average viewing figure of Top 10 programmes viewed in 1990: 17.62m

Rank	Programme	Date	Channel	Audience (millions)
1	Neighbours*aggregated, lunchtime+teatime showing	26 Feb 1990	BBC1	21.16
2	Coronation Street	01 Jan 1990	ITV	19.20
3	Only Fools and Horses	25 Dec 1990	BBC1	17.97
4	It'll Be Alright on the Night	01 Dec 1990	ITV	17.92
5	Film: E.T.	25 Dec 1990	BBC1	17.50
6	Film: A View To A Kill	31 Jan 1990	ITV	16.93
7	The Generation Game	25 Dec 1990	BBC1	16.73
8	World Cup 1990: England v West Germany	03 Jul 1990	BBC1	16.69
9	Inspector Morse	w/e 28 Jan 1990	ITV	16.16
10	World Cup 1990: England v Ireland	11 Jun 1990	ITV	15.96

[online] **http://www.barb.co.uk/facts/since1981?year=1990&view=top10**

[13] Barb. Since 1981. Top 10 Programmes

BARB Top 10 UK TV Programmes 2008 [accessed 18 February 2010]
Average viewing figure of Top 10 programmes viewed in 2008: 13.26m

Rank	Programme	Date	Channel	Audience (millions)
1	Wallace and Gromit: A Matter Of Loaf and Death	25 Dec 2008	BBC1	16.15
2	The X Factor Results	13 Dec 2008	ITV1	14.06
3	Britain's Got Talent Final Result	31 May 2008	ITV1	13.88
4	The X Factor	13 Dec 2008	ITV1	13.77
5	Doctor Who	25 Dec 2008	BBC1	13.10
6	Coronation Street	18 Jan 2008	ITV1	13.02
7	Strictly Come Dancing	20 Dec 2008	BBC1	12.97
8	Dancing On Ice	16 Mar 2008	ITV1	12.08
9	Britain's Got Talent	30 May 2008	ITV1	11.86
10	EastEnders	24 Mar 2008	BBC1	11.73

[online] **http://www.barb.co.uk/facts/since1981?year=2008&view=top10**

[14] McKinsey report: (2006) Boosting returns on marketing investment, *Profiting from Proliferation*, ed APWebb *et al*, pp100–01, McKinsey & Company, New York.

> *'Fragmenting media and changing consumer behaviour are exposing the limits of the traditional model. Consider the following trends.*
>
> *Media proliferation. In the United States, the original handful of TV stations has proliferated into more than 1,600 broadcast and cable TV outlets. Similar trends are underway in Europe.*
>
> *Multitasking. While surfing the Web, the typical US teenager engages in an average of two other activities, one of which is often homework (exhibit 1). Some 80 percent of business people also multitask*
>
> *Switching off. Consumers are increasingly selective about what they watch and the advertising messages they trust. According to Yankelovich Partners, 65percent of them feel "constantly bombarded with too much advertising," 69 percent are "interested in products and services that would help skip block marketing," and 54 percent "avoid buying products that overwhelm with advertising and marketing."*
>
> *By 2010, we estimate, television advertising in the United States could be only 35 percent as effective for some as it was in 1990. Many European countries are likely heading down a similar path. And while the impact of recent trends on B2B marketing is harder to measure, it probably will be similarly dramatic as common marketing vehicles (such as direct mail, sponsorship events, trade magazines, and sales forces) become less effective'*

[15] Brandgymblog.com 'Advertising is a tax for having an unremarkable product' November 28, 2006 [accessed 1 February 2010]:

> *'This quote is by Robert Stephens, Founder and "Chief Inspector" of the Geek Squad, from his speech at last week's Marketing Society Conference in London. He has been able to grow his computer repair business from a one-man start-up to a company employing 15 000 "agents" in the USA, and secure a UK launch with Carphone Warehouse, all without the need for advertising. How? By designing every single bit of the Geek Squad experience to maximize impact and create word-of-mouth.'*

[online] **http://wheresthesausage.typepad.com/my_weblog/2006/11/advertising_a_t.html**

Chapter 03

[1]   International Marketing Conference on Marketing & Society, 8–10 April, 2007, IIMK. *The Dark Side of Relationship Marketing* D. Ramkumar, S. Saravanan [accessed 25 February 2010]:

> 'For academicians it is a paradigm shift in marketing philosophy urging the importance of long term relationship and retaining existing customers over getting new customers; since a bird in hand is better than the two in a bush. For practitioners Relationship marketing is a competitive advantage..., a tool to reduce the customer churn..., a tool to overcome service failures..., an opportunity for marketing additional products and services to a more receptive customer base....
>
> Evolution of Relationship Marketing. In 1983 Leonard L. Berry, distinguished professor of Marketing at Texas A&M University, coined the word Relationship Marketing when he presented a paper entitled Relationship Marketing at the American Marketing Association's Services Marketing Conference. The paper was published in the conference proceedings and for the first time the phrase Relationship Marketing appeared in the Marketing literature.'

[online] **http://dspace.iimk.ac.in/bitstream/2259/340/1/453-457.pdf**

[2]   Webreference.com. What is RSS [accessed 25 February 2010]:

> 'Really Simple Syndication (RSS) is a lightweight XML format designed for sharing headlines and other Web content. Think of it as a distributable "What's New" for your site. Originated by UserLand in 1997 and subsequently used by Netscape to fill channels for Netcenter, RSS has evolved into a popular means of sharing content between sites (including the BBC, CNET, CNN, Disney, Forbes, Motley Fool, Wired, Red Herring, Salon, Slashdot, ZDNet, and more). RSS solves myriad problems webmasters commonly face, such as increasing traffic, and gathering and distributing news. RSS can also be the basis for additional content distribution services.'

[online] **http://www.webreference.com/authoring/languages/ xml/rss/intro/**

Chapter 04

[1] JFK Library. Inaugural Address of President John F. Kennedy.
Washington, DC. 20 January 1961. John F. Kennedy Presidential Library
& Museum [accessed 1 March 2010]:

> '...And so, my fellow Americans: ask not what your country can do for
> you – ask what you can do for your country. My fellow citizens of the
> world: ask not what America will do for you, but what together we can
> do for the freedom of man.'
>
> [online] **http://www.jfklibrary.org/Historical+Resources/Archives/**
> **Reference+Desk/Speeches/JFK/003POF03Inaugural01201961.htm**

[2] New Media Age. Changing habits make it harder to gauge web user
sophistication. 8 October 2009. Robin Goad, director of research,
Experian Hitwise UK [accessed 1 March 2010]:

> 'At the start of the millennium, when internet use was much lower than
> today, a good way of measuring someone's online sophistication was
> to ask if they'd bought something online. But now more of us are online
> more often and with faster connections, there has been a key change in
> the way we use the internet.
>
> Just three years ago transactional sites received 5% more UK visits
> than those offering content like news and entertainment; today content
> sites get 73% more traffic than shopping sites, and the gap continues
> to widen.'
>
> [online] **http://www.nma.co.uk/opinion/industry-opinion/changing-**
> **habits-make-it-harder-to-gauge-web-user-sophistication/**
> **3005305.article**

[3] Problem Maps® were first introduced in Grant Leboff's 2007 book, *Sales
Therapy®. Effective selling for the small business owner*, Capstone
Wiley. They are available for download at www.stickymarketing.com.
Problem Maps®.

Chapter 05

[1] About.com.:Economics. The Post War Economy: 1945–1960. The Post
War Economy: 1945–1960. From US Department of State [accessed 14
March 2010]:

'...During the 1950s, the number of workers providing services grew until it equaled and then surpassed the number who produced goods. And by 1956, a majority of U.S. workers held white-collar rather than blue-collar jobs.'

[online] **http://economics.about.com/od/useconomichistory/a/ post_war.htm**

[2] Economy Watch. Economy, Investment & Finance Report. Advantages of the Service Economy [accessed 14 March 2010]:

'...IBM is an unique example. In spite of being a manufacturing company it tends to call itself a services company. This has been the scenario since it realized that the price elasticity of demand for business solutions is less elastic than for hardware. The company now benefits from the revenue of the elongated contracts rather than receiving payment in a single mode.'

[online] **http://www.economywatch.com/economy-articles/ service-economy.html**

[3] Ford. About Ford. The Model T Put the World on Wheels. Mass Production Begins [accessed 22 June 2010]:

'In October 1913, mass production of the Model T began at Ford's Highland Park, Michigan, Assembly Plant. Henry Ford had previously organized men and components to enhance Model T production, but the moving assembly line quickly improved chassis assembly speed from 12 hours and eight minutes to one hour and 33 minutes. In 1914, Ford produced 308,162 cars, more than all other automakers combined. It was also in 1914 that the Model T, in the interest of streamlining production, was no longer available in red, blue, green or grey; it was now available in "any color so long as it is black." '

[online] **http://www.ford.com/about-ford/heritage/vehicles/ modelt/672-model-t**

[4] New Media Age. The X Factor attracts 1.75m Facebook fans. Tue, 15 Dec 2009. By Mark Banham [accessed 15 March 2010]:

'The X Factor has proved a social media success story for ITV, with 1.75m Facebook fans and 59,000 Twitter followers, according to figures released today by the broadcaster and its online content partner, TalkbackThames Digital. Nearly 20m TV viewers tuned in to watch Joe McElderry snatch The X Factor title and a £1m recording contract, cheered on by mentor Cheryl Cole. Social networking shared in the

success, with 1.75m fans of the series on various Facebook pages and 20,000 Facebook app downloaded. Up to 50,000 comments were recorded on the social network each weekend of the competition. This was accompanied by 59,000 Twitter followers and 230,000 live comments on ITV.com by the end of the series.'

[online] **http://www.nma.co.uk/the-x-factor-attracts-175m-facebook-fans/3007885.article**

Chapter 06

[1]   Wikipedia. Unique Selling Proposition [accessed 15 March 2010]:

'The Unique Selling Proposition (also Unique Selling Point) is a marketing concept that was first proposed as a theory to explain a pattern among successful advertising campaigns of the early 1940s. It states that such campaigns made unique propositions to the customer and that this convinced them to switch brands. The term was invented by Rosser Reeves of Ted Bates & Company. Today the term is used in other fields or just casually to refer to any aspect of an object that differentiates it from similar objects...

Definition. In Reality in Advertising (Reeves 1961, pp 46–48) Reeves laments that the U.S.P. is widely misunderstood and gives a precise definition in three parts:

1) *Each advertisement must make a proposition to the consumer. Not just words, not just product puffer, not just show-window advertising. Each advertisement must say to each reader: "Buy this product, and you will get this specific benefit."*

2) *The proposition must be one that the competition either cannot, or does not, offer. It must be unique—either a uniqueness of the brand or a claim not otherwise made in that particular field of advertising.*

3) *The proposition must be so strong that it can move the mass millions, i.e., pull over new customers to your product.'*

[online] **http://en.wikipedia.org/wiki/Unique_selling_proposition**

[2a] Netbooks 2008. Engadget. ASUS Eee PC given away with T-Mobile mobile broadband package. By Darren Murp. Posted May 8th 2008 9:12AM [accessed 15 March 2010]:

'We're calling this right now: ASUS' Eee PC is the new MP3 player. But only in the context of giveaways. Anyhow, just days after RBC announced that it would dish out free subnotes if prospective customers joined in, PowerUp Mobile is now offering a similar deal for UKers who sign up for T-Mobile's Web n Walk mobile broadband package. In short, folks comfortable with inking their name on a two-year contract at £35 per month will net a free USB modem and a Eee PC 2GB Surf. Better hurry – the deal expires on June 15th.'

[online] **http://www.engadget.com/2008/05/08/ asus-eee-pc-given-away-with-t-mobile-mobile-broadband-plan/**

[2b] Netbooks 2009. PC World. Office Hardware. July 06, 2009 2:00PM. Netbooks Offered Virtually Free With Mobile Contracts. By Agam Shah, IDG News Service [accessed 15 March 2010]:

'Netbook prices in the U.S. are tumbling as retail stores are offering the machines virtually for free, but with caveats attached to them. Retail store Best Buy is selling Hewlett-Packard's Compaq Mini 110c-1040DX netbook, which has a 10-inch screen, for $0.99, but with a two-year mobile broadband contract from wireless carrier Sprint. The contract limits subscribers to 5GB of Internet data usage per month, with extra fees if the limit is exceeded. Sprint's 3G mobile broadband plans start at around $60 a month. HP's netbook is available without a contract for $389.99. Consumer electronics store RadioShack is offering an Acer Aspire One with an 8.9-inch screen for free with a two-year AT&T mobile broadband contract, according to the retailer's Web site. AT&T's 3G mobile broadband plans start at $60 a month. RadioShack's offering goes on "while supplies last." The netbook is priced at $349.99 without the contract. Both netbooks have basic configurations, making them good for word processing and Web surfing, but weak on graphics capabilities… Telecom providers started offering netbooks with wireless contracts last year in Europe and Asia, which helped spike the shipment numbers of the low-cost devices. The trend reached the U.S. late last year, when RadioShack announced it would offer an Acer netbook for $99 with a two-year mobile contract from AT&T. Worldwide netbook shipments totaled around 11 million in 2008, with the number expected to double this year, according to research firm IDC. Netbook distribution through telecom companies has found a sweet spot in Western Europe, where telecom companies have accounted for 25 *percent to a third of the netbook shipments, said David Daoud, research manager at IDC.'*

[online] **http://www.pcworld.com/businesscenter/article/167929/ netbooks_offered_virtually_free_with_mobile_contracts.html**

[3] How Stuff Works. Publications International, Ltd, the Editors of. "21 Best-Selling Books of All Time." 14 September 2007 [accessed 15 March 2010]:

Publications International, Ltd, the Editors of. "21 Best-Selling Books of All Time."

Title/Author	Copies Sold (millions)
1 *The Bible*	5,000–6,000
2 *Quotations from Chairman Mao Zedong* by Mao Zedong	900
3 *The Qur'an*	800
4 *Xinhua Zidian*	400
5 *The Book of Mormon* by Joseph Smith, Jr.	120
6 *Harry Potter and the Sorcerer's Stone* by J. K. Rowling	107
7 *And Then There Were None* by Agatha Christie	100
8 *The Lord of the Rings* by J. R. R. Tolkien	100

Title/Author	Copies Sold (millions)
9 *Harry Potter and the Half-Blood Prince* by J. K. Rowling	65
10 *The Da Vinci Code* by Dan Brown	65
11 *Harry Potter and the Chamber of Secrets* by J. K. Rowling	60
12 *The Catcher in the Rye* by J. D. Salinger	60
13 *Harry Potter and the Goblet of Fire* by J. K. Rowling	55
14 *Harry Potter and the Order of the Phoenix* by J. K. Rowling	55
15 *Harry Potter and the Prisoner of Azkaban* by J. K. Rowling	55
16 *Ben Hur: A Tale of the Christ* by Lew Wallace	50
17 *Heidi's Years of Wandering and Learning* by Johanna Spyri	50
18 *The Alchemist* by Paulo Coelho	50
19 *The Common Sense Book of Baby and Child Care* by Dr. Benjamin Spock	50

Title/Author	Copies Sold (millions)
20 *The Little Prince* by Antoine de Saint-Exupéry	50
21 *The Mark of Zorro* by Johnston McCulley	50

[online] **http://www.howstuffworks.com/ 21-best-selling-books-of-all-time.htm**

[4] Coca-Cola. Our Company. Operating Group Leadership [accessed 15 March 2010]:

'Javier C. Goizueta is Vice President, The Coca-Cola Company, and President of the global McDonald's Division. He leads a worldwide organization that is responsible for building the strategic alliance with McDonald's in over 31,000 restaurants located in 119 countries.'

[online] **http://www.thecoca-colacompany.com/ourcompany/bios/ bio_113.html**

[5] Virgin. About Virgin [accessed 15 March 2010]:

'Virgin is a leading branded venture capital organisation and is one of the world's most recognised and respected brands. Conceived in 1970 by Sir Richard Branson, the Virgin Group has gone on to grow very successful businesses in sectors ranging from mobile telephony to transportation, travel, financial services, media, music and fitness.

Virgin has created more than 200 branded companies worldwide, employing approximately 50,000 people, in 29 countries. Global branded revenues in 2008 exceeded £11 billion (approx. US$17 billion).

We believe in making a difference. Virgin stands for value for money, quality, innovation, fun and a sense of competitive challenge. We deliver a quality service by empowering our employees and we facilitate and monitor customer feedback to continually improve the customer's experience through innovation.'

[online] **http://www.virgin.com/AboutVirgin/WhatWeAreAbout/ WhatWeAreAbout.aspx**

Chapter 07

[1]   You Tube. Susan Boyle – Singer – Britain's Got Talent 2009. YouTube [accessed 17 March 2010]:

> *'89,144,015 views'*

>   [online] **http://www.youtube.com/
>   watch?v=9lp0IWv8QZY&feature=fvw**

[2]   Business Week. Viewpoint January 18, 2008, Advertising: Now a Conversation by Ted Shelton [accessed 17 March 2010]:

> *'…In a 2006 study, researchers found that only 53% of consumers said they believed ads were a good way to learn about new products. That was down from a 78% response in 2002.'*

>   [online] **http://www.businessweek.com/technology/content/jan2008/
>   tc20080117_870338.htm**

[3]   Mark Shaw. Twitter and customer service – Starbucks Style. 2010 January 31. By Mark Shaw [accessed 17 March 2010]:

> *'It is fair to say, that I do love a latte. In fact I would say that I am addicted to them. It is rare that a day goes by, without my fix of a good latte. For the last 18 months or so, I have been a massive Costa Coffee fan. In fact, I think that I have probably single handedly put Costa Coffee Barnet on the map. I talk about them so much, that I am sure that most peeps think they pay me, or I have shares in their business. Both of which I can state are not true… Every day, I talk about Costas in Barnet, I have many of my business meetings in there, and the Oxford Circus branch, and yes I do like their latte's. I am very well known by their staff, and over this time, have often suggested ideas to them on how to improve things. I have also contacted them via Twitter… And the result… Nothing. Nada. Zero response. I am an amazing customer for them, I have not added up what I have spent over the last 18 months, but a latte 5 days per week, at least 3 almond croissants each week, and many a toasted sandwich… all must add up to a fair amount… Enter Starbucks. So there I was on Sunday having just collected my daughter Jessica. She lives near to London Colney, so we often go to the Starbucks in Sainsburys, have a drink, she has a marshmallow twizzler, and then we buy a few things in Sainsburys. This morning was no different, I sat down for my drink, and tweeted.*

Approx 3 mins went by... when I checked my phone, I noticed that I had received a message from Starbucks, in fact it was from the MD of Starbucks UK and Ireland... Darcy Wilson–Rymer. Now imagine how I felt... 18 months blasting Costas, spending a fortune, talking about them, being a top customer... and in one message they may well have lost me. During the course of the day, myself and Darcy exchanged more messages. He seemed genuinely interested in me, and experience of his brand. Exactly as I would have hoped. He wanted to know what I thought of his shops, and was all ok. Now I don't know about you, but to me that is what great customer service is all about. Oh and don't forget the most important thing... What have I now done, I have written about my experience and will tell others... They have created a great advocate for their brand, and all in 1 message that may well have taken Darcy 10 seconds...

Never, never underestimate great customer care and service. Oh and Costas, I really do hope that you are reading this blog post, but somehow, I strongly doubt it....'

[online] **http://www.markshaw.biz/ twitter-and-customer-service-starbucks-style/**

[4] Gonintendo. Wii marketing blitz – the rundown. November 13 2006 by RawmeatCowboy. Ambassador Program [accessed 17 March 2010]:

'Hands-on Sampling

Wii Ambassador Program: The yearlong initiative identified ambassadors in markets throughout the country. These ambassadors are of three categories: multigenerational families, hard-core gamers and modern moms. During the initial phase, Nintendo hosted events for each ambassador and 30 of his or her closest friends and relatives. The events offered an opportunity for everyday people from all walks of life to play Wii for the first time and share their experiences with others.'

[online] **http://gonintendo.com/viewstory.php?id=8448**

Chapter 08

[1] BBC News. Monday, 20 December, 1999, 18:37 GMT. Martian ad a Smash hit. Smash hit: The 1970s aliens won the ad industry's heart too [accessed 18 March 2010]:

'A TV commercial for mashed potato featuring a group of talking robotic Martians has been named advertisement of the year by a trade magazine. Advertising weekly Campaign named the 25-year-old Cadbury's Smash commercial its favourite in its top ten of the century. The spots featured the creatures chortling as they heard how the "Earth people" peeled their own potatoes, "boiled them for 20 of their minutes," then "smashed them all to bits" – instead of using Smash instant mash. Viewers were not insulted at being called "a most primitive people" by the metallic creations – sales soared and the Martians received so much fan mail the agency which made the commercials, now known as BMP DDB, had to prepare special literature to reply to them. Now BMP DDB is celebrating the accolade by showing the original 1974 commercial in Channel 4's final advertising slot of the year at 2355 GMT on 31 December.'

[online] **http://news.bbc.co.uk/2/hi/entertainment/572903.stm**

[2] Wikiquote. Sir Winston Leonard Spencer-Churchill, KG, OM, CH, TD, FRS, PC (Can) (1874-11-30–1965-01-24) was a British politician. He was Prime Minister of the United Kingdom from 1940 to 1945, and again from 1951 to 1955. He received the Nobel Prize for Literature in 1953 [accessed 18 March 2010]:

'"For my part, I consider that it will be found much better by all Parties to leave the past to history, especially as I propose to write that history." Speech in the House of Commons (January 23, 1948), cited in The Yale Book of Quotations (2006), ed. Shapiro & Epstein, Yale University Press, p. 154, ISBN 0300107986. This quote may be the basis for a statement often attributed to Churchill: "History will be kind to me. For I intend to write it."'

[online] **http://en.wikiquote.org/wiki/Winston_Churchill**

[3] Daily Record. Man sues Lynx after failing to pull in seven years. Oct 31 2009 Ben Spencer [accessed 18 March 2010]:

'A LUCKLESS Romeo has sued cosmetics firm Lynx after he failed to land a girlfriend during seven years of using their products. Indian Vaibhav Bedi, 26, is seeking £50,000 from parent company Unilever for the "depression and psychological damage" caused by the lack of any Lynx effect. Court officials in New Delhi have accepted dozens of half-used body washes, shampoos, anti-perspirants and hair gels for forensic tests. Lynx – marketed as Axe in India – is famous for its saucy ads showing barely clothed women throwing themselves at men.

Vaibhav said in his court petition: "The company cheated me because in its advertisements, it says women will be attracted to you if you use Axe. I used it for seven years but no girl came to me." Unilever refused to comment on the case.'

[online] **http://www.dailyrecord.co.uk/news/weird-news/2009/10/31/ man-sues-lynx-after-failing-to-pull-in-seven-years-86908-21786843/**

Chapter 09

[1]   Companies House. UK: Company Registrations. Companies In Data Management Information [from an e-mail supplied 1 March 2010]:

'Year:1990–91; 1,186,900'

[2]   Companies House. UK: Company Registrations. Companies In Data Management Information [from an email supplied 1 March 2010]:

'Year 2008–09; 2,722,700'

[3]   US Census Bureau. 1992 Statistics of U.S. Businesses (SUSB) Data US businesses: All Industries – 1992 [accessed 2 March 2010]:

'Establishments; 6,319,300'

[online] **http://www.census.gov/econ/susb/data/susb1992.html**

[4]   US Census Bureau. 2006 Statistics of U.S. Businesses (SUSB) Data US businesses: All Industries – 2006 [accessed 2 March 2010]:

'Establishments; 7,601,160'

[online] **http://www.census.gov/econ/susb/data/susb2006.html**

[5]   Guardian. Cafepress: Jack Schofield, 18 August 2008 [accessed 25 December 2009]:

'Not many shops stock 150 million products. Cafepress not only manages this amazing feat, it adds around 45,000 new ones every day. This is only possible, of course, because the products don't exist until someone orders them. Your T-shirt, poster, cap, bag, book, mug or whatever is produced and shipped on demand.

But that is only half the Cafepress story. The other half is that its business is based on that old Web 2.0 standby, "user-generated content". Instead of buying a T-shirt printed with someone else's design, you can create your own. And if it's really good, you might even make a bit of money by letting Cafepress sell it to everybody else. If you fancy trying your hand, you can set up a small business using Cafepress to collect the money, produce the goods, mail them out, and handle customer service. All you need is access to a computer and some graphics software that can save your design in, for preference, the PNG (portable network graphics) format. The site provides web space and has a Learning Center to help you get going.

Cafepress, founded in a garage in 1999, has now grown to the point where it has more than "6.5 million independent shopkeepers and members in addition to syndicated and corporate stores", including geek favourites Dilbert and Wikipedia.'

[online] **http://www.guardian.co.uk/technology/2008/aug/18/ cafepress/print**

[6] Time. Top 10 Websites 2007 By Catherine Sharick # 1Lemonade.com [accessed 7 Jan 2010]:

'Making extra cash through lemonade-stand sales isn't just for kids anymore. You, too, can now get in the game at Lemonade.com by setting up a virtual "stand" filled with products you'd recommend to friends. Add the widget to your Facebook, MySpace or blog pages and when purchases are made through your site, you receive 5% to 15% of the cost of the item. The stands are a win–win for everyone: Online retailers get free advertisements, social networkers are recommended good products, and you get paid if the deal goes through.'

[online] **http://www.time.com/time/specials/2007/top10/article/ 0,30583,1686204_1686305_1691135,00.html**

[7] Lemonade. Current Total, Lemonade stands [accessed 1 March 2010]:

'43097 Total'

[online] **http://www.lemonade.com/marketplace/**

[8] eBay. Who we are. Overview. E-commerce [accessed 1 March 2010]:

'With more than 90 million active users globally, eBay is the world's largest online marketplace, where practically anyone can buy and sell practically anything. Founded in 1995, eBay connects a diverse and passionate community of individual buyers and sellers, as well as small businesses. Their collective impact on e-commerce is staggering: In 2009, the total worth of goods sold on eBay was $60 billion – $2,000 every second.'

[online] **http://www.ebayinc.com/who**

[9] IT PRO. IE slips as Chrome continues to gain market share. And today's launch of the IE browser ballot looks likely to continue the decline. By Nicole Kobie, 1 Mar 2010 at 10:01 [accessed 2 March 2010]:

'Internet Explorer has slipped again as Chrome is the only browser to post a gain in market share this month, according to Net Applications.

"The Google Chrome browser gained 0.4 per cent of global usage share in January. All other major browsers showed a month-to-month decline," the analytics firm noted.

Chrome now holds 5.61 per cent of the market share, and the third ranking after knocking Apple's Safari from that spot in December. Google has been advertising heavily to encourage users to try its browser. Microsoft's Internet Explorer holds 61.58 per cent, down just slightly from 62.12 per cent in January, while Mozilla's Firefox slipped from 24.43 per cent to 24.23 per cent.'

[online] **http://www.itpro.co.uk/620980/ ie-slips-as-chrome-continues-to-gain-market-share**

[10] Wikipedia. Search traffic. Alexa. About Wikipedia (wikipedia.org): An online collaborative encyclopedia [accessed 7 February 2010]:

'Percent of global Internet users who visit wikipedia.org: 13-Jan-2001. 3 month: Reach 12.558. Change +24.88%'

[online] **http://www.alexa.com/siteinfo/en.wikipedia.org/wiki/ Main_Page#**

[11] Wikipedia. Statistics. From Wikipedia, the free encyclopedia [accessed 7 February 2010]:

'Page statistics. Content pages 3,186,767. Pages (All pages in the wiki, including talk pages, redirects, etc.) 19,376,508. Uploaded files 867,442'

[online] **http://en.wikipedia.org/wiki/Special:Statistics**

[12] Wikipedia. List of Wikipedias. From Meta, a Wikimedia project coordination wiki [accessed 7 February 2010]:

'All 272 Wikipedias are ordered by article count. The table lists each language name in English (linked to the English Wikipedia entry for the language) and the "local" name, in the language itself (linked to the article in that language's wiki).'

[online] **http://meta.wikimedia.org/wiki/List_of_Wikipedias# Languages_without_ISO_639_language_code_or_duplicated_or_ using_incorrect_code**

[13] Gartner. The Gartner Fellows Interview. Author and Futorist Alvin Toffler. Alvin Toffler was interviewed by Gartner Fellow Ken McGee on November 27, 2006 [accessed 22 June 2010]:

> 'We invented the word prosumer many years ago in my book The Third Wave. It's a composite of production and consumption, obviously, and we argue that there was, prior to the invention of money, people who lived without money. Everybody was a prosumer, growing their own lunch, sewing their own clothes, building their own shack and so on. So it was a pre-monetary or a nonmonetary economy. However, more and more prosuming populations (moved over to) become part of the (consuming or) money system.'
>
> [online] **http://www.gartner.com/research/fellows/ asset_165710_1176.jsp**

[14] History. This Day in History. Music. Mar 6, 2001: The death spiral of Napster begins [accessed 27 March 2010]:

> 'In the year 2000, a new company called Napster created something of a music-fan's utopia—a world in which nearly every song ever recorded was instantly available on your home computer, for free—. Even to some at the time, it sounded too good to be true, and in the end, it was. The fantasy world that Napster created came crashing down in 2001 in the face of multiple copyright-violation lawsuits. After a string of adverse legal decisions, Napster, Inc. began its death spiral on March 6, 2001, when it began complying with a Federal court order to block the transfer of copyrighted material over its peer-to-peer network.
>
> Oh, but people enjoyed it while it lasted. At the peak of Napster's popularity in late 2000 and early 2001, some 60 million users around the world were freely exchanging digital mp3 files with the help of the program developed by Northeastern University college student Shawn Fanning in the summer of 1999. Radiohead? Robert Johnson? The Runaways? Metallica? Nearly all of their music was right at your fingertips, and free for the taking. Which, of course, was a problem for the bands, like Metallica, which after discovering their song "I Disappear" circulating through Napster prior to its official release, filed suit against the company, alleging "vicarious copyright infringement" under the U.S. Digital Millennium Copyright Act of 1996. Hip-hop artist Dr. Dre soon did the same, but the case that eventually brought Napster down was the $20 billion infringement case filed by the Recording Industry Association of America (RIAA).'
>
> [online] **http://www.history.com/this-day-in-history/ the-death-spiral-of-napster-begins**

[15] BBC News Channel. Page last updated at 06:02 GMT, Friday, 16 January 2009. Legal downloads swamped by piracy [accessed 10 February 2010]:

'Ninety-five per cent of music downloaded online is illegal, a report by the International Federation of the Phonographic Industry (IFPI) has said.'
[online] **http://news.bbc.co.uk/1/hi/technology/7832396.stm**

[16] Digital Daily. iTunes: 10 Billion Songs Sold in Less Than Seven Years. by John Paczkowski. Posted on February 24, 2010 at 3:30 PM PT [accessed 27 March 2010]:

'Apple (AAPL) launched the iTunes Music Store in the U.S. in April of 2003. By the end of the year, it had sold more than 25 million songs. By February 2006, that number had risen to one billion. Now, just four years later, it's passed another landmark: 10 billion songs sold. Astonishing – more so, when you recall that it was just 18 months ago that Apple was crowing about crossing the five billion songs sold threshold.

"This has been the birth of legal downloading," Apple CEO Steve Jobs said of iTunes when it first launched in 2003. "We're going to fight illegal downloading by competing with it. We're not going to sue it. We're not going to ignore it. We're going to compete with it. With iTunes you're supporting artists. You're not stealing. It's good karma.'
[online] **http://digitaldaily.allthingsd.com/20100224/ apples-itunes-thanks-10-billion/**

Chapter 10

[1] iTunes Store.AroundMe [accessed 10 February 2010]:

AroundMe allows you to quickly find out information about your surroundings. How many times have you found yourself in need of finding the closest Gas Station? AroundMe quickly identifies your position and allows you to choose the nearest Bank, Bar, Gas Station, Hospital, Hotel, Movie Theatre, Restaurant, Supermarket, Theatre and Taxi. AroundMe shows you a complete list of all the businesses in the category you have tapped on along with the distance from where you are. For every listing you can choose to see its location on a Map, view the route from where you are, add the information to your contact list or even email the information to a friend. The Nearby listing allows you to find information using Wikipedia about what is around you.'

[online] **http://itunes.apple.com/us/app/aroundme/
id290051590?mt=8#**

[2] Foursquare. Share your experiences with friends [accessed 10 February 2010]:

'Think of foursquare as an "urban mix tape." We'll help you make lists of your favorite things to do and let you share them with friends. Think beyond your standard review – we're looking less for "The food here is top notch" and more for "Go to Dumont Burger and try the most amazing Mac and Cheese ever." Foursquare will keep track of the things you've done, help you create To-Do lists and even suggest new experiences to seek out. As you check-in around the city, you'll start finding tips that other users have left behind. After checking-in at a restaurant, it's not uncommon to unlock a tip suggesting the best thing on the menu. Checking-in at a bar will often offer advice on what your next stop should be. Every tip you create is discoverable by other users just by checking-in.'

[online] **http://foursquare.com/learn_more**

[3] Mobile Marketing Magazine. August 19, 2009. The Channel Balancing Act [accessed 10 February 2010]:

'Darren Ponsford, Strategy and Planning Director at Blueview Group, argues that in today's world, offering consumers channel choice, and then learning which channels they prefer for which activities, is vital.
Channel choice. Offering consumers channel choice does more than provide a platform for companies to speak with their customers – it helps gain their business in the first place, and then ensure their ongoing loyalty. This finding comes through loud and clear in a survey of 2,000 UK consumers commissioned by Blueview. If a UK company does not offer communication choice, then potential buyers are much less likely to purchase its products, and existing customers are much more likely to switch to a competitor. The survey showed that, when considering buying from companies they have never bought from before, 66% of UK consumers said they would be extremely unlikely to buy from a company that does not offer them their preferred channel of communication. And 61% said that if a brand they currently use failed to offer them choice of channel, they would look for a competitor that

does. In other words, at the most basic level, marketers need to make multiple communications options available, and find out what those favoured channels are across their customer base.'

[online] **http://www.mobilemarketingmagazine.co.uk/2009/08/ the-channel-balancing-act.html**

INDEX

NB: page numbers in *italic* indicate figures or tables